Praise

'The Price Writer nine-step method ... a clear and compelling description of what you need to get right to be great at leading a pricing team. Jeremy has written a book that is thought-provoking as well as a treasure trove of insight and ideas for both current and aspiring leaders in general insurance pricing. I will keep a copy close to hand to make sure I keep focusing on the right things and avoiding those all too common pitfalls!'
— **James Hillon**, Pricing Leader

'At a business conference, I heard this wise saying, "To navigate the path, one must have a comprehensive view of the terrain." This perfectly captures Jeremy's successful effort to collect, organize and explain the bigger picture of insurance pricing and I am extremely happy that finally someone did that. Whether you're embarking on your initial journey as a pricing analyst or already in a top role, this book is a perfect match for you. Throughout ten chapters you will be elevated above the details of modelling and have an insightful view of other crucial aspects of insurance pricing such as strategy, team dynamics, deployment, portfolio monitoring and more. Each chapter is enriched with authentic narratives, useful best practices, and thought-provoking exercises to contemplate your own scenarios. Enjoy your path!'
— **Dawid Kopczyk**, CEO of Quantee

'Becoming a successful pricing leader takes a very different skill set to that needed to be a great pricing analyst. As an industry we have often struggled to help our analysts bridge this gap and step up to the leadership challenges we face in a changing world. In this book, Jeremy provides an original and comprehensive guide to pricing leadership for UK General Insurance. *Price Writer* will be a vital resource for both existing and new pricing managers alike.

'Jeremy's approach is much more than a theoretical guide; it's a practical companion. Jeremy sets out clear, actionable steps and uses case studies relevant to an analyst's journey towards leadership, with many real-world examples similar to those I have experienced many times over my own career. He interweaves these with the broader dimensions of pricing and offers holistic insights on strategy, governance and team dynamics essential for leadership in this field.

'I will be recommending this book as key reading for my future pricing leaders, and whether you are a seasoned or new manager I hope you will enjoy and use this book.'

— **Andy Cooper**, Director of Pricing at esure

'Jeremy Keating has written a unique, focused guide to pricing excellence in general insurance that provides strategic and tactical advice relevant for pricing teams globally. On almost every page, Jeremy's depth of experience shines through as he shares hard-won lessons across data management, pricing modelling and team leadership, among other areas. I highly recommend this book for pricing analysts and leaders looking to embed best practices in their teams and executives who want to take their pricing operations to the next level.'

— **Ronald Richman**, Pricing Leader, Old Mutual Insure

PRICE WRITER

THE NINE-STEP METHOD
TO BECOMING A HIGHLY
SUCCESSFUL GENERAL
INSURANCE PRICING LEADER

JEREMY KEATING

R^ethink

To my father, Robert Keating.
I know that you would be proud of this book
and jumping around telling everyone.
I love you and miss you every day.

Contents

Foreword

In insurance, it seems that all roads lead to pricing.

Better pricing is the strategic lever to profitability, growth, fraud prevention and footprint control, as well as avoiding trouble with the regulator. As a consequence, pricing teams – and their remit – have grown immensely during my decade or so in general insurance.

When I started out, pricing roles were more about verifying the underwriters' decisions with data, dazzling the business with Excel skills, and reporting on the written footprint. Now, a successful pricing team can no longer confine itself to building good risk models annually: it must take the lead on finding and actioning market insight; set governance processes that stay ahead of ever-changing regulatory regimes; define systems that are capable of storing vast quantities of data from an array of sources; build and deploy increasingly complex statistical models that are updated with increasing frequency; drive realistic business plans and the accompanying reporting; and they must make all of this appear sensible and explainable to both customers and the wider business.

No one is as cognisant of this change than Jeremy. In this book, Jeremy not only defines a successful pricing team, but challenges you to become one too. This is not a staid academic textbook, but a holistic and practical view of pricing, from data systems to post-deployment monitoring.

The speed of change in insurance pricing means that almost everyone working in it has some knowledge gaps, and this book is refreshingly open about that. Whether it's setting up your data tables or how to communicate errors to the wider business, product knowledge or the intricacies and pitfalls of working with date fields, this book will remind you what you don't know and give you practical steps on how to correct that. Whether you are the Chief Pricing Officer, a new manager or an analyst trying to understand the bigger picture, this book offers insights that will challenge and support your development as a pricing professional.

On the face of it, insurance pricing is very simple: charge customers the right price for their level of risk. Of course, we know that the reality is complex and interesting, demanding and exciting. So too with this book: it is short and simple to read but poses questions that are not always straightforward to answer.

Insurance, and therefore its pricing, is going to change further and faster over the next decade. It has new challenges to face and new problems to discover. There is no single correct answer, but this book has a lot of the right questions that you will need to be asking to improve your team, your data, your processes and your results, whatever lies ahead. Leading a great pricing team is not easy. But if your experience, knowledge, curiosity, pragmatism and – let's face it – sheer tenacity has brought you this far, then welcome.

This book is for you.

Catrin Townsend, GI Pricing Manager and author of *A Risky Business*

Introduction

In *Zero to One* Peter Thiel challenges the reader to think of something they know to be true but which few other people agree with.[1] Here's mine: vertical progress in general insurance (GI) pricing has almost ground to a halt. Let me explain. Vertical progress means successfully doing something new, or as Peter Thiel would call it, going from zero to one. Horizontal progress is the proliferation of something successful that people are already doing, that is to say going from one to n.

To verify this we need to think about the innovations we've seen in the past. At the end of the eighties, scientific pricing using data analysis emerged, and this was the first time algorithmic models were

---

1   P Thiel and B Masters, *Zero to One* (Currency, 2014)

used to individualise prices. Prior to this there was little granularity in pricing – it was largely a single rate for exposure, based on human knowledge and so-called expert judgement. Since then we have had only horizontal progress in modelling. Modelling has proliferated and new modelling methods have been used, but all of that takes us from one to n, not from zero to one. It is only horizontal progress.

Data has become readily available, and it is often held in high-quality data tables. IT infrastructure is always improving, allowing us to do ever more computationally demanding work: we have added external data and external knowledge to the pricing process; we've brought governance into pricing; deployment is often done inside of pricing teams by pricing specialists. Our capabilities have jumped massively. Science, computing and statistics have replaced almost all other disciplines in pricing teams, and those teams have access to powerful reporting and high-quality pricing tools.

Horizontal versus vertical progress

It is true that, through these innovations and others, vertical progress has been made, despite the fact that pretty much every time new ideas are implemented they are resisted. In the past, vertical progress has won; however, over the decades of my life so far I've seen things proliferate outwards in horizontal progress to multiple insurers and providers, and that horizontal progress is still going on. There are parts of the market that have adopted these things, parts that have not, and parts that are going through that transition now. Clearly, the horizontal proliferation of science and reason in pricing continues, as all markets and parts of markets will adopt science-led pricing. Those that resist continue to be placated with lines like 'It's assisting them to set prices' while the march of horizontal progress continues.

People might point to machine learning and other developments in modelling, but these are just ways of doing the modelling better. They are not new, but improving on what is already successful – going from one to n. The same applies to telematics – it is undoubtedly useful but it's more external data – and to parametric, although one could call that the opposite of progress.

We need to make vertical progress.

At least 99% of us are engaged in making horizontal progress: we're proliferating the things we already know are successful. The fact that the insurance sector can somehow manage a multi-decade resistance to scientific pricing despite it being patently better, shows how unwilling the industry is to embrace improvements and innovations. Insurers, with their huge capital, can still survive with rates dreamed up in the mind of one person, despite the fact that the rest of the world is governed and driven by algorithms.

We need more than 1% of us to be engaged in making vertical progress. We need to ask how we put new things in place, things that someone isn't already doing. It's easy to do things a little better; it's hard to succeed at doing new things.

Some might say there's secret innovation going on. It is a good point, but could genuine vertical innovation in pricing really be kept secret? A company that has true innovation in an area no one else knows about would have obviously better long-term results than the others. Most continue in the pricing arms races with horizontal progress, and some fall by the wayside. Some manage good results for a period, though often these seem to end with claims reserve strengthening. Where there is progress it seems horizontal, not vertical.

Vertical progress has stalled, stagnated, and stopped.

My journey

When I was first promoted to pricing management, I was profoundly excited to have gained the success I had desperately craved for a long time, but I found the change in my role difficult and disorientating. There was so much I didn't know, but the training I went on as a new manager was unhelpful. None of it was about the problems I had; it was either so general that it was useless for being a leader in a technical role or super specific on technical work which didn't relate to the work I did or help me to manage my team. It was the same old story of 'What got you here will not get you there'.[2] I struggled in the new role and it took me a long time to find my feet and become the leader I am today.

We want our pricing leaders to become the most successful and highly valued leaders in GI and I do not want others to struggle like I did. We need to provide the knowledge and skills for them to excel in the work they do. My goal is to see every pricing leader reach the level that matches their ambition; I don't want anyone to give up early with their potential unfulfilled.

In his book *Be Useful*[3] Arnold Schwarzenegger tells a story about helping people to achieve. He recounts a time when he was asked to introduce a class of people to weightlifting.

There was one young man who found it impossible. Just before they finished, Arnold asked him if he wanted to try again. He managed several lifts with Arnold adding a small amount of weight each time.

When they stopped, the young man jumped up and the rest of the group started celebrating his win. Arnold said he saw the young man gain strength and grow in confidence right before his eyes.

---

2   M Goldsmith, *What Got You Here Will Not Get You There* (Hachette, 2007)
3   A Schwarzenegger, *Be Useful* (Penguin, 2023)

It's an amazing feeling, a joy that fills you, when you see other people win. This transformation is what I want to see for you, and my hope with this book is that you will experience the same joy as that young man when you start to achieve your goals.

How this book will help

This book is necessarily about horizontal progress. It's about improving. It's about the proliferation of what is successful. By following the steps in the book, you will become highly valued. There is also a challenge woven through the book, a challenge to myself and to you. Innovate to go from zero to one. Do something differently. Make vertical progress.

The proliferation in the number of people involved in pricing, hundreds in individual companies, may look like evidence of progress but it's evidence of the opposite: the grinding arms race that we find ourselves in because we're mainly making horizontal progress and not vertical advancements.

If you're a GI pricing person with the ambition of becoming a leader, or if you're already an insurance leader overseeing pricing, then this book is for you. I'll help you to:

- Understand how to help your teams to make and deploy quality prices correctly and on time

- Put the right people in the right positions

- Ensure that your team has the right skill set and know how to retrain them if not

- Implement and integrate the data set-up, IT infrastructure and pricing software that's right for your organisation

I will answer some of the biggest questions in GI pricing and set out a clear process for helping pricing leaders achieve their ambitions. A pricing leader's biggest fear is failing at their sales and loss ratio goals, and that fear can be broken down into nine areas, which I'll cover in chapters one to nine in this book.

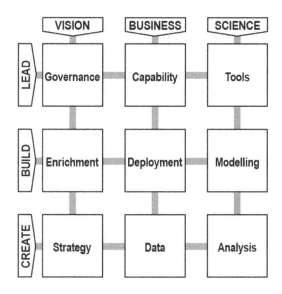

Pricing leaders don't write computer code. The programming and statistics you learn on the job are more than enough, and if you're putting time into learning more, then that's commendable but it won't advance your career. Why do people spend time learning those things? Simply because it's easier to learn more detail about something familiar than to grow by learning new things they might find hard.

To succeed, you need a combination of the following three things:

1. Something the world wants

2. Something you are good at

3. Something you love

I can help you with this and I can even help you to be better paid for doing it. I might be able to help you rediscover what you love about it, but the passion for it has to come from you. You need to enjoy what you do because a lot of the time it's going to be hard, and it's your passion that will keep you going through the tough times.

PART ONE
VISION

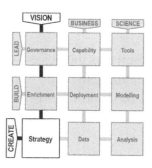

1

Strategy

I f a pricing leader cannot tell you in one word (or at the most one sentence) what their price strategy is, then they do not have one. As well as being able to clearly articulate the price strategy briefly and succinctly it should also be communicable as one paragraph, one page, and one document depending on the detail needed for the audience. In this chapter I'll explain why you need a price strategy and why it needs to be the bedrock of your pricing team if you want to be highly valued and recognised.

What is a price strategy?

Many people misunderstand what a price strategy is. Firstly, it is not what you are trying to achieve – that is known as the objective. Secondly, it is not the detail of the things you do – those are tactics. A price strategy is the high-level principle that summarises how you achieve the objective.

Example price strategies include:

Accuracy	Equitable	Responsive
Adaptive	Explainable	Scalable
Approvable	Fairness	Simple
Clarity	Innovative	Skimming
Competitive	Long-term value	Sophisticated
Consistent	Loss-leading	Stable
Cost-plus	Mutualised	Telematics
Cross-subsidised	Optimised	Value
Dynamic	Penetration	
Economy	Precision	

If the leader doesn't have a strategy, the team doesn't have a strategy and will not have clear direction. This is the root cause of almost all difficulties in getting the best out of your team. Symptoms may include conflict and disagreements, mistakes, miscommunication, missed deadlines, indecision, low productivity and lack of trust.

I have often seen multiple team members each with a different direction, each prioritising their own values when they produce their part. This means there is a clash when setting the prices together, like the proverbial 'too many cooks'. Different people and teams put their own values in the prices, and so the whole is not consistent and does not match up to the organisation's values and strategy, leading to frustration both within and outside of the pricing department.

A price strategy can be referred to when decisions need to be made. Although it does not mean foregoing other principles, it makes clear what the guiding principle for the department will be. If scalability is in the price strategy it does not mean, for example, sacrificing fairness. Fairness can still be the objective or one of the things you do, but the way you operate should be scalable and this includes your approach to fairness.

All strategies exist to solve problems, to communicate the choices people should make when confronted with options, to allow people to adapt to new situations consistently and in alignment with the rest of the company's behaviour and to decide in advance what are optimal courses of action in future. When we look at successful companies and teams, we should generally be able to work out their strategy.

Here are some examples from the wider world:

Apple = Quality

Google = Relevance

IKEA = Affordability

SpaceX = Reusability

Toyota = Efficiency

Here are examples from insurance:

Admiral = Experience

Direct Line = Personalised

Ping An = Technology

State Farm = Community

Zurich = Innovation

Each of these strategies solves problems and allows people and teams in the organisation to make choices that align with the company's optimal behaviour.

What is the purpose of the pricing department?

The pricing department exists as a conduit between the company's goals and the customer's pocket. Company goals come in two flavours. Firstly, there are the financial goals in the organisation's financial plan, and secondly, there are the softer values of the company which are focused on its mission and vision. The pricing team is key to achieving both.

The financial goals are often quite clear, in that the pricing team needs to set prices that achieve a certain amount of premium and have a level of profitability. It's much harder for the pricing team, which is typically made up of numbers-focused people, to translate the work it does into the softer values around how the business operates.

A soft goal might be that the organisation wants to be committed to and make a positive contribution in the lives of customers, or to project confidence and stability, or to create community for the team. Making pricing part of achieving these hard and soft goals is important for the whole organisation.

A pricing team within, say, a supermarket is different from a pricing team within an insurance company. A supermarket's pricing team are looking for a single, viable price to charge every customer in the country, or at least in the local area. They know at the outset what it costs to stock the product and that cost is the same for every customer. Customers are homogenous and the pricing team can see demand at different price levels for the whole group. The price is visible to every customer.

Insurance pricing is the opposite in almost every way. The pricing team does not know at the outset what it will cost to offer the product, it does not cost the same for each customer, customers are heterogenous, prices are not immediately visible to customers and measuring demand is complicated.

The insurance pricing team must decide segmented pricing on an individual basis for every customer. For insurers, who are often painted as not being individualised when it comes to customers, it's stunning to see just how individualised creating a price for a particular person is.

If the insurance company just wants to generate a certain amount of revenue from each of its customers, it could simply divide the amount of money it wants by the number of customers it has; however, the reality of doing this is that it will only sell where it is cheaper than its competitors. Those competitors know that the price is too low, and so this approach is not viable.

A pricing team exists so that an insurer can be competitive, sustainable and compliant with regulations. Being slightly better in pricing than everyone else has a massive advantage. If an insurer knows just one more piece of information than everyone else about a customer, this knowledge enables them to position themself in a way that makes them more profitable overall.

Avoiding anti-selection and moral hazard

The real reason a pricing department exists is to solve a problem that is conceptually quite simple but in practice exceedingly complex: to avoid anti-selection and moral hazard; that is, to find the right price for every individual customer – what I call the 'Goldilocks price', the price that's just right. This price is not the same for every organisation. It is the price that is just right for that customer for your product from your company.

Depending on your organisation, you may be looking to achieve profitability from a customer in a short period of time, you may want to maximise the number of renewals the customer will make with you, or you may be putting fairness at the heart of your business – in each case, you're thinking about the price that's exactly right to achieve these objectives from each customer. Achieving what the business wants while not being selected against and not promoting moral hazard is what the pricing department is for. This is why it's so important to encourage discussion and buy-in from stakeholders and to think about how pricing reflects organisational goals.

Customers generally expect parking their car in a garage to result in a lower premium; however, statistics may show that people who park their car in a garage need a higher premium, which comes as a surprise to them, particularly when they change that information when asking for a quote.

The pricing team is then put in an awkward position. Do you set the price that might please expectations or the one that results in you being profitable? If everyone else is going to charge people more for parking in a garage, then you also have to because if you go against the flow on that, you'll lose money. If you are the only one who charges the right price then you are selecting against your competitors, making you profitable and them not. There is no choice. You have to charge the customers who say they park in the garage the higher price. You have to follow the statistics and bring expectations with you.

There are other surprising factors that affect insurance premiums. For example, it might be that for a customer living in a Neighbourhood Watch area, they are likely to pay more, not less, in premiums. It could be the same with burglar alarms. People with burglar alarms might pay more for their insurance because they've got things that are worth protecting. Originally, people got burglar alarms to reduce their insurance premiums, but it was discovered that when people with burglar alarms are burgled their claims are more expensive because they have more valuable possessions. The higher claim cost offsets the lower incidence of burglary, so people with burglar alarms should be charged more than people without. An insurer has to do this; if they don't then they are selected against or miss the opportunity to select against their competitors.

Anti-selection is about doing what the data tells you to do. If this goes against the flow then you win; if it goes with the flow then you don't lose. You lose when you do the opposite of what the data says you have to do.

Making business fair

People often think that the function of the pricing team is to ask customers more and more questions, and that's perceived as a problem, so you should try to find out the information you need through enrichment instead.

When you make your prices accurate, what generally happens is that some customers pay more and some pay less than they used to. Every time the pricing team collects more data, you start coming to the heart of what 'fair' means, and when it comes to fairness there are two extremes: you remain completely mutualised and charge everyone the same amount, or you individualise and have a price strategy where different people pay different amounts.

Mutualising your pricing is only going to work in a situation where the government makes every insurer charge the same amount, and of course some people would consider that to be a fairer way of working out premiums. When you individualise, you have a situation where people only pay the amount they deserve to pay, and many people consider this to be the fairer approach. Insurers are then faced with a philosophical problem, because you can argue that either way of deciding pricing is fair.

I prefer the individualised approach because you are not using one group to subsidise another, which creates a situation where some people are paying more than they should to fund those who are paying less. Ultimately this comes down to behaviours. If you know that no matter how you behave, you're going to pay the same amount for your insurance, then there's no incentive to be healthier, a better driver, protect employees, make sure you secure your property, or follow a host of other good behaviours.

That's where the moral hazard part comes in. When you neutralise prices, it's a negative for society because more of society's resources are then spent on paying for unnecessary accidents and poor behaviours. Plus the human cost. The same applies to driving if you adopt a one-size-fits-all pricing policy. An individualised system is fairer and also better for society as a whole, but it's not without issues. You can see this with younger drivers in particular. My nephew got a quote for insuring his first car and the cost of the insurance was more than the car's worth.

It's important to never lose sight of the fact that one of the most important functions of the price strategy is to give clarity to people in and outside of pricing.

This is because when people know what their role is, it helps them to be proud of the work they're doing and to be loyal to the organisation they're with. We don't often talk about staff in terms of them being followers, but in some ways they are. It's much easier to follow someone who's told you what they believe in, what they're trying to achieve and what they want from you as an employee.

This strategic approach with pricing shows everyone in the organisation that the pricing team is not just about the maths, it's also about values. When you can communicate that to people, you stop having to look at every decision and analyse it deeply. When you know what your values are, you can say 'No, that's not the kind of thing we do' or 'That's right for us because it aligns with what we're trying to achieve.'

When formulating your price strategy, you need to make sure you keep in mind what the point of the strategy is. You want to create something that's easily understood, and you need to ensure that the pricing team, and everyone in the organisation, know what they are trying to achieve and how you will achieve it. You need to take your time over it and put real effort behind it because getting it right at the start will save you effort later on. There are five stages to developing and implementing the strategy.

1. Identify

The first stage is to meet with the pricing team and have a conversation about their needs, then use your findings to identify who your stakeholders are in the business. It's then vital to meet with each of the stakeholders to ask them about their individual needs. There shouldn't be an agenda behind the meeting; it is an opportunity to take time to really listen to what each stakeholder has to say. Stakeholders need to see that the strategy made in the boardroom lives on in the price strategy too and that the price strategy is enacted on the ground, so you need to get feedback from them to understand what they want from you. You should also try to imagine what customers would say their needs are. Ask one of the teams that is close to your customers to feed back to you what customers say.

Generally, the stakeholders you need to meet with include the following:

- Strategy leader
- Compliance leader
- Underwriting team
- IT department
- Claims department
- Customer service department

- Product leader

- Finance leader

It's also worth talking to HR and communications. They might not have a great deal of input, but you definitely want to get them into the meeting as they will be responsible for communicating the resulting strategy throughout the organisation, and they will do this much more effectively if they've been present during the strategic planning stage.

2. Define

After these meetings, you define the identified needs in the form of needs statements. Try to make each need distinct, and where they cross over from different teams combine them into one statement. A good statement consists of a situation and a desire, which can be high level or specific. For example, 'When a customer changes their details leading to a price change, I need prices to move in a way that is explainable to the customer', 'When setting prices, I need every customer to pay a positive margin over the lifetime of their policy', 'When a customer renews their policy, I need them to consider price to be a key reason to stay with us', 'When deploying price changes, I need to understand the impact of the changes' or 'When reviewing previous price changes, I need to know if we are achieving expectation or deviating from our plan'. Poor statements would include 'I need pricing to sell more polices', 'I need us to have low prices', 'We need to increase revenue', 'We must hit our plan' and 'We need accurate impact analysis'.

Any needs that conflict with each other or with what pricing can achieve should be noted for feedback. Conflict often arises between profitability and customer experience, between growth and sustainability, and between anti-selection and customer or stakeholder expectations.

Take the needs and try to put them into groups based on what they are about, possibly trying to match this to the way your company divides up its overall strategy or mission statement. You want to end up with a basic framework, ideally with between three and five pillars that contain the different types of need; for example, they could be about financials, service, fairness or customers.

3. Prepare

Having defined the needs, it is time to prepare the goals, which should be solutions to the needs. The aim is to boil down the needs to the smallest possible number of goals that encompass all of the needs. You want the price strategy to be short and easily understood. The example needs above could be covered by these goals:

- Differences in prices between groups should be understandable, supported by data and explainable.

- The expected customer margin should be positive over the lifetime of a policy.

- Price changes at renewal should be within certain limits defined by clear criteria and well understood.

- After deploying price changes, those changes should be reviewed to understand the impact and make sure lessons are learned from any deviations.

- Impact analysis is presented to your governance structure with sufficient information for them to make informed decisions on the financial and customer outcomes.

4. Confirm

Having prepared a draft price strategy with the goals in a logical framework, it's then time to confirm it with the other pricing leaders and with the stakeholders. The indemnified needs that conflict will have to be discussed with the relevant teams, and it is your responsibility to draw a compromise and explain what can and can't be done. You need to take the time with the different stakeholders because if you settle them into something they agree with today, then later on down the road you can refer to the strategy for the reason why you're choosing a particular course of action. It's then so much easier to get buy-in from them: they've already bought into the high-level strategy, so they'll be happier with the detail when it's communicated to them.

5. Execute

After these meetings, you should end up with a price strategy that your department and stakeholders support. You should formally agree it within your governance structure and I recommend doing this to the highest appropriate level, which could be sign-off at your board. I also recommend doing this swiftly after your stakeholder meeting while it is still fresh in everyone's minds.

You must avoid ending up with a document which is then forgotten about. You need to make sure that the price strategy is live and embedded within the department. You should also include adherence to the price strategy in your audit and governance activity; it needs to be something you truly live by to satisfy both your department and your organisation. When new people join your department, they should be taken through the strategy. It should be referred to in your departmental meetings, and it should be used to design activity, report progress and set objectives for the year. When you feel you have talked endlessly about the price strategy it will have started to become embedded.

Ask your stakeholders to answer the following questions:

1. What do you need from a pricing team?

2. What do you want us to be achieving and how do you see us working well together?

3. What is a good set of prices for you?

You won't be able to satisfy everyone, of course, but taking the time to manage that relationship and getting stakeholders to eventually agree to something that might be a compromise between teams is an important part of the exercise, as is getting stakeholders to understand the needs of the rest of the organisation. When everyone understands the goals and the part they play in achieving those goals, they work more effectively. Constantly ask yourself if what you and the team are doing is moving you towards achieving the goals in the price strategy.

A good example of this would be an insurer who wants to build a price strategy by taking their company strategy and turning it into something the pricing team can work with. To do this my company would meet with the pricing leaders and then the outside department heads. We would crunch all of the information together to come up with a price strategy they can use. We map parts of the corporate strategy to the aims of the pricing team to end up with a strategy that can be understood by everyone within the organisation. Even someone who'd just joined as a graduate pricing person could read the price strategy and understand it.

EXERCISE: Preparing a successful price strategy

1. Identify the needs of the pricing team and your stakeholders.
2. Define those needs in a coherent framework.
3. Prepare goals that encompass delivering each of those needs.
4. Confirm with the pricing team and your stakeholders that these goals do meet their needs.
5. Execute the price strategy as the DNA of everything you do.

Summary

I've explained why a price strategy is important, and the difference between the objective, the strategy and the tactics. The objective is what we are trying to achieve, the tactics are the things you do to achieve the objective, and the strategy is how you operate. The strategy can also be thought of as what you orientate yourself and the department around.

Strategies exist to solve problems and to aid people and teams in making choices that match up with the company's optimal behaviours. They make it so leaders can ensure their team make the right choices when confronted with multiple options. This is a way of optimising the team without needing to micromanage choices. With a clear strategy that can be communicated easily, your people will always know how they should work to align their output with the optimal way of working across your team and department.

We have looked at the purpose of the pricing team and why in a competitive market it is essential to individualise prices. This is to avoid anti-selection and moral hazard. These are both poor for you and your company financially. They are also detrimental to customers and society as a whole.

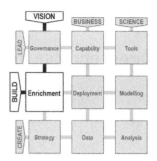

2
Enrichment

I n this chapter I'll talk about how you can navigate your many options for enrichment and strengthen your position with information obtained from outside the pricing department. I'll discuss data and why it's so important to capture and organise it in the correct way. I'll also explain why you need experts on the things you underwrite and why it's so important to listen to those experts and include their knowledge, which may be qualitative, in your prices.

There are two types of enrichment, direct and indirect.

Direct enrichment

This is what you use to set prices, so it determines what those prices are. Examples of direct enrichment are:

- Geographical attributes
- Sociodemographic data
- Credit- and customer-specific data
- Proof of identity
- Property attributes
- External frequency and severity predictions
- Climate, weather and wildfire data
- Flood data
- Susceptibility to subsidence or other ground issues
- Market premiums
- Property value tables
- Crime information
- Past insured events such as crime, fires or accident data
- Energy usage
- Journey times

- Telematics data

- Internet of things (IoT) devices, including to detect flood and fire, to monitor usage, security and environment, and wearables and trackers

Direct enrichment divides itself into several different types. A common one is static data, which consists of things you can look up and make a table of, so called because the information doesn't change quickly. Sometimes you may enrich prices using a prediction based on static data; for example, a forecast of the market price or of flood risk. Census data is a good example of static data. Another form of direct enrichment is 'looked up' information, or lookups. This is where the information is tabular in nature but changes fairly rapidly, so the lookups need to be directly linked to the providers of the data. This could be information about someone's driving licence or their credit details.

You still need the information you collect from the policyholder, which provides the foundation of the prices you set, but you need to supplement that with additional information. Different countries are at different places with adopting external data. In the UK we're good at using information about customers that we take from external sources; for example, private providers like credit reference agencies give us a lot of useful information about people.

Accurate price setting

Accurate price setting leads to better loss ratios and bigger books. An example relates to address verification: an insurer who finds that a small number of policies fail address verification and that group is responsible for a disproportionately large amount of claim costs. So a stunning amount of money is spent on a small group of customers. Simply closing the door to people when their address can't be verified would result in a significant profit increase.

There are a number of different places you can obtain direct external data from. There are data brokers, who typically collect lots of information and sell it on. That can be quite a simple approach because you only need to do one lookup to get lots of information. LexisNexis and Experian are quite common in this regard. There are also individual data providers who specialise in supplying a specific piece of information which might be a lookup. Lookups are now the most common form of direct enrichment in the UK, although there are still some providers who will give you static tables.

Gathering data

There have been more barriers to adopting external data sources in Europe and the US than in the UK, and often this is due to the granularity of the data available. This is changing, with a plethora of providers now offering quality and granular data on many potential pricing factors. As an example from vehicle insurance, many countries have a government body for licensing with data on every vehicle and every driver. In some countries that information is readily available, in others availability is developing.

The adoption of the IoT and telematics has been quite slow in the UK, as it has been in a lot of Europe. The US is far ahead of us where vehicle telematics is concerned, and a high percentage of policies are now informed by external data that's collected directly and sent to the insurer. Pay-as-you-go policies require monitoring how often the customer is driving so that they can be charged appropriately, thereby providing a way to enrich pricing data.

Telematics and IoT devices rely on the customers wanting the product, or at least on showing them that there is some benefit to taking the product and providing their data. This needs to be over and above what they would get from a product without monitoring. For example, usage-based pricing works well because the customer sees a benefit from only paying when they use the product, but you can only get that data if you can offer your customers a worthwhile product in exchange for providing their data. You can make direct decisions based on the pricing, but you can also make underwriting decisions, such as declining to renew a customer if you feel their driving is not at the standard you need it to be.

Customers can obtain smoke alarms and water loss devices that can notify them or the insurer of issues, and this information can then be used in your pricing. You want to have a more comprehensive understanding of the risk, but there are many things you can't ask the customer directly because they either wouldn't know the answer or they wouldn't know it to the accuracy you need. As I mentioned above, it's also poor customer care to ask hundreds of questions – the customer is likely to get tired and not bother to pursue you as an insurer. Being able to get that information externally is of huge benefit.

If you're going to insure someone against flood, for example, nothing can beat a quality flood assessment by flood experts, and understanding the granularity of this is even more important. The geographic area and number of properties within a postcode (aka zip code) greatly varies between counties. They're small in the UK, but even so it's easy to imagine a postcode on a hill where the property at the bottom could have a much higher flood risk than a property at the top. Getting that granularity right down to the individual property matters, and that's relatively easy to do in the UK, although there is a cost associated with that.

It's a similar scenario with vehicles: it's relatively easy to pick up information from the codes that go with a vehicle make and version, but there's nothing quite like getting the specific information about a particular vehicle; for example, knowing how many owners it's had and its history. Once again, there are usually costs involved in finding out this type of granular information, but it's powerful when used to set your prices.

There are several avenues that insurers can go down to source external data during the insurance pricing process. Here are a few examples:

- **Data brokers** specialise in collecting and selling data from a variety of sources.

- **Telematics** involves using sensors and GPS technology to collect data.

- **IoT devices**, such as detectors and cameras, can collect data.

- **Data providers** are specialists in particular types of data and provide this properly in packages so it can be used for insurance pricing.

The challenges of using external data

There are of course challenges associated with external data. It provides insights, but you need to think about the data quality, particularly with external look-ups but also with static tables. The data will go out of date and it may not always be reliable, so you need to carry out due diligence on the providers of your data to ensure that it's accurate and usable.

There are privacy concerns too. You need to make sure your own terms and conditions allow you to do these lookups and also that you make customers aware of any areas where you might have to do this. You may need special permissions and agreements to use some external data. There's also the physical integration of the data to consider. How do you make it work in your pricing engine? Even with static data, that can be quite difficult if many sources or large tables are being used.

In your live rating environment, you need to have the items you're going to use as a key to look things up. It could be the address, or the customer's licence number or registration. You need to verify they've entered the correct details and you can't ever be absolutely sure they have. Addresses are particularly complicated as they come in so many different formats. A lot of good work has been done in recent years to clean these up, particularly online when people select their addresses from a drop-down menu. This is much more controlled than it once was, but even so you can still have problems. You'll need to find the unique identifiers from those addresses or other references to then join on to other data, and that can mean you have lots of tables in your live environment. In the modelling chapter, I'll show you some ways to reduce that complexity.

The online external data comes with similar challenges. You have to physically send out requests for information to the data broker or the data provider, and some requests will come back without an answer. The broker or provider can't possibly have every record, so you need to work out ways of handling those unknowns. People expect online quotes to be returned extremely quickly, particularly if they're using a price comparison website, and so you have to ensure you can deliver at speed. Your IT infrastructure should return those prices in split-second timing, including external lookups.

This is quite a challenge and there is a cost involved. A surprisingly huge amount of data is available for free, but the granular stuff comes with a cost attached. Progress has been made towards paying when you sell a policy rather than on each lookup, and this could be particularly good for smaller providers. Every company should have an external data policy as part of its governance structure, and that policy should be well embedded into the pricing team. You need to keep logs, and when you add or update data, you need to undertake assessments of it to make sure it meets regulations and fits with the ethical approach of your organisation.

Indirect enrichment

Indirect enrichment covers all the information that insurers obtain from outside sources that's used in pricing but not directly setting an individual customer's price. That is, it supplements the internal data you hold and therefore the direct enrichment. It is where you use other information, or your own knowledge, to enrich your prices. Indirect enrichment comes in many flavours, as I will outline in the examples below.

Exposure benchmarking

In many countries it is possible to obtain quality data on the population; for example, the number of vehicles of different makes and types that are registered in a country. Comparing the mix of the full population proportions with the mix of the proportions of what has been written and is being written in a book of business shows whether there is a tendency for certain segments to be over- or under-represented (aka exposed), which uncovers anti-selection or overly cautious rate setting. To do this it is necessary to reweight the population based on the underwriting footprint. Benchmarking can also be invaluable for expanding the underwriting footprint and setting prices to do so successfully, especially when an insurer may have little or no other data on a new segment.

Research

Indirect enrichment includes studying the thing that's being insured. This could mean looking at reports to do with, for example, electric vehicles, but it could also include looking at information about properties or liability to learn more about the things you're insuring. If multiple reports come out – for example, an inflation report or statistics from the relevant bodies, or a report about changing trends – that information will inform your indirect enrichment.

Expert views and opinions

Speaking to experts and training pricing staff to be knowledgeable about the items they are insuring is new. When I started, the prevalent thought at the time could have been summed up as 'It doesn't matter what we are insuring, the maths would apply if it was rubber bands snapping.' That has since been superseded. You can improve your prices through subject matter knowledge by consulting experts and learning about what you are insuring.

While it was once the purview of underwriting and claims specialists to know about the insured items, and underwriters would study and learn a great deal of information about what they were insuring, it is now important for the pricing team to share that knowledge. Underwriting has been in decline as a profession for a number of years and that trend is accelerating, so it's becoming normal to see the pricing team as the new experts. They should be getting serious knowledge about the items they insure to make sure they're setting sensible prices and have good external reports.

Taking the time to speak to experts and learning from experts, even employing them or having them regularly address your staff, can significantly boost people's knowledge, particularly when you get to the hard mathematics. To return to the example of electric vehicles, at the moment we can see that the world is changing with their arrival. In the UK we are committed to a future where all new vehicle sales are electric cars, and other countries have similar aims. From that time onwards, there won't be any new internal combustion cars manufactured, so vehicle insurance is changing and we need to change our approach. Currently, we don't have the data to do this, so we need to speak to, and learn from, the experts.

Deciding on the use of factors, or what levels to group in a line of business, can be enhanced by talking to experts. Think about enrichment: when you use statistical significance levels, such as testing at 5% confidence intervals, one in twenty times you will end up accepting something that doesn't deserve to be there, and having expert knowledge can make the difference in weeding out these flukes.

Inflation

Inflation is also important. High inflation may come and go but inflation is a fact of life. Statistical agencies can tell you what inflation was, but you can only forecast inflation or rate the value of other people's forecasts if you understand the drivers of inflation. You can use past data as an anchor, but it doesn't tell you what you need to charge in the future. The more you study the claims environment, the better you can understand what you need to know in the future, the better you can be at this, and the better placed you'll be against your competitors. It's important to obtain these external reports so that you can look at supply chains and get an idea of what's going to happen in the future.

EXERCISE: Strategies to support indirect enrichment

1. Write down the things you would like to know about policyholders but which you don't currently receive information on.

2. Think about and investigate whether there are people who could provide you with that data. Surprisingly often the answer is yes.

3. Ask yourself some vital questions, such as 'What would happen if my competitors knew that information and I didn't?'

4. Do some research to find out what free information you might be missing out on and set up some processes to sensibly test the significance of new data. The faster you can test stuff and work out whether it will be useful, the more you can do and the more effective your rating will be.

5. Consider the following questions:

   • When was the last time you spoke to an expert about the things you're insuring?

- When did you last have someone external come and address yourself or your team about the things you're insuring?
- When did you last share your prices with an external expert and ask them for their opinion?

Summary

Enrichment comes in two flavours: direct and indirect. The point of enrichment is to improve the accuracy of our prices by enhancing what we know about the customer, their situation, the item being insured and other risk and pricing factors.

Direct enrichment includes information that is looked up live during the rating process so that it is instantly up to date. It also includes information that changes less often and so can be taken from offline sources and static tables. Indirect enrichment includes reports and external information. It is also about seeking expert guidance and teaching yourself and your team about the items being insured and the relevant processes. We can use external data to benchmark our own position. For example, comparing the mix of your exposure to the mix of the total population or our prices to the market price for a similar policy for a similar customer. This gives us powerful tools for setting our prices and controlling our exposure. Through indirect enrichment you can know where you sit compared to competitors and the wider world and then take the right actions to get to where you need to be to achieve your objectives.

Taking some time to think about the questions I've posed will help you understand where your organisation is in relation to its enrichment journey.

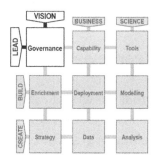

3
Governance

In this chapter we'll look at governance and why it's so important to carry out the correct procedures to ensure you have effective governance across your organisation, and I'll discuss the checks you will need to carry out to confirm you have the correct safeguards in place.

Effective governance has to start at the lowest level and go all the way up through the pricing team to the most senior level of the organisation. You need to have the right people working in each area and making the right decisions at each level of governance.

Peer reviews

What we would call the lowest level is also the most detailed level where an analyst is writing code and setting prices. The first important aspect of working at this level is to have work reviewed by a peer, ideally someone with a similar, or a slightly more developed, skill set than the person doing the work. It's not enough to just review models, because they are only one part of the process. Other parts of the process, including coding, data, analysis, formulas and documentation, need to be appropriately reviewed too. Most problems arising at this level are due to poor or nonexistent peer reviews on coding. Examples of this include:

- **Miscalculations** – Fields that are derived from information like exposure are calculated incorrectly.

- **Incorrect joins** – Items like claims data are joined inappropriately so they end up being duplicated or entered at incorrect time periods.

- **Incorrect keys** – Tables are matched incorrectly at the wrong granularity or to the wrong items.

- **Mismappings** – Factors and features are set to the wrong levels.

- **Reconciliation** – There is no proof that the data is correct unless it reconciles well to other sources and to itself.

- **Blanks and unknowns** – Features and factors end up with unknown levels when they are in fact known.

- **Precision and formatting** – Information is lost due to rounding, data type changes or formatting issues.

Coding often isn't checked properly and this is usually a systemic problem. We've moved at quite a pace in the last fifteen to twenty years. Different languages and different systems have evolved, so it's not unusual to find people in the hierarchy who can't check the coding of people who work for them, which is quite a detailed task. This is because either they don't have skills in that particular language or system or they know the language but haven't used it for a long time.

Ideally, you want to have a system in place whereby one person does the work, another person checks that work (usually someone at roughly the same skill level) and then a manager reviews what's been done to check the work's been completed properly. There have to be thorough reviews of coding. Surface checks and glances over what has been done are not enough. Genuine checks and reconciliation should be part of the DNA of all teams that do this work.

Manager reviews

The next level is systematic checking. When you want to make changes to the business, you need a hierarchical structure to decide which areas have the right knowledge and skills to sign those off. A system I've seen work well is when organisations start at the top and delegate authority downwards. If you ask people at the top level 'How much authority are you comfortable with giving to someone below you?' it raises the question of how much they are willing to let other people decide and how much they feel needs to come to them personally. It's a regulated industry where the person at the top, the officer of the company, is ultimately responsible for the work that's done below them, and so everyone needs to be clear on the remits of their particular role.

It's not unusual to reach a point where people say they do not want authority to be delegated to them or it is obvious that they are not senior or experienced enough to be trusted with that authority. From that point upwards in the hierarchy there should be a committee structure. The people with delegated authority should be given advice and help from people in their own and other areas. A system that works well is to have a technical committee largely made up of pricing people who can properly challenge the work done in other areas. They get into the detail and ensure there is real ownership of achieving accurate and correct prices. Then there is a higher-level committee over this and so on up to the top.

Departmental reviews

Once you've had peer reviews and manager reviews you'll want to implement departmental reviews. You'll need to present the work openly and honestly and listen to challenges from other areas. It's important to make sure people have enough resources and bandwidth to properly attend to and challenge these other areas. It's also fairly common to want external challenge at this level. This is the first level where you'll want someone involved who is from outside of the department but who's skilled in pricing. Finding someone who's a genuine outsider but who has the right skill set to join your technical committee can make a huge difference to the quality of challenge and will both reduce the number of mistakes and improve the quality of work. What works well is when you have someone who operates in a way similar to non-executive directors on boards. Remember that this person is exclusively for pricing; removed from the team structure, they do not have any regard for the politics but have the position and skills to provide real insight and challenge.

This all goes back to what I said at the beginning of this book: if you get the right processes, the right systems and the right people in place at the beginning, everything rolls out in a much simpler, easier and less stressful way. Ultimately the role of the leader is to build the processes and the structures and the team.

Creating committees

The following order of seniority typically works well:

1. A technical committee to control the details of how prices are made. They decide how things should be done before those things become prices.

2. A pricing committee to ensure things have been done correctly before they are implemented and to oversee the structure and implementation of the rates.

3. A product committee to oversee the delivery of the financial plan.

4. Higher-level governance to agree the price strategy and the financial plan.

The technical committee

The technical committee is, naturally, one that can debate a lot of detail. Problems with the approach should be raised here when they come up to ensure price setting remains well controlled. The technical committee should have a core membership of the senior people from the pricing team. It could also be helpful to seek help from other experts at times when their skills are appropriate; for example, a media expert could be helpful when considering what methods are appropriate, as they can opine on how methods could be viewed by the outside world, such as in the media, by customers or by regulators. Compliance experts can act similarly and also help with advising on controls over data, methods or other considerations.

The technical committee should approve and keep records of technical aspects of the work; for example, what methods have been agreed on for creating and setting prices and what data is acceptable for use in directly setting the customers' prices. The committee should agree on pricing policies that make these requirements clear, which can be used by the pricing team and others to understand how prices are being set. It should also set procedures to ensure those rules are followed. An important aspect of this is keeping logs on what data and methods are acceptable.

Policies could cover things like selecting data sources, assessing enrichment, choosing model features and setting price adjustments. Your teams can do almost any investigations they wish, but what ends up in a customer price must meet the rules set by this committee.

The pricing committee

The pricing committee controls what is deployed. When a proposal is made to the pricing committee, there should be evidence that the rules of the technical committee have been followed. There should be no need for the pricing committee to debate small details like what exact rate adjustments are being made, as these are controlled through the policies of the technical committee. The pricing committee could have a role in overseeing the technical committee's policies, but it depends on whether this is felt appropriate and what delegated authority is held by the members of the technical committee. The important point is that how things are done must be well understood before work is completed so the pricing committee can focus on results and driving forward with good controls over that work. This ensures there are good controls and good debate in the right circumstances at the right times.

It is sensible to also have a regular meeting, monthly or quarterly, that includes discussion on pricing, underwriting, claims and reserving. This needn't involve a formal committee and can be used to present information from other committees, but it is a place to openly discuss the emerging claims experience, the movements in past experience and what is expected in the future. It is an opportunity to review the figures in a technical but not necessarily formal setting, thereby ensuring all parties are aware of each other's general position. It can also be used to update on work and projects.

In the pricing committee it is important to hear views from a wider part of the business. You'll want to have representation from areas like underwriting, sales, claims and compliance and you need to be open with your pricing proposals. Sometimes you'll need to educate others on the narrative because not everyone will understand the complex maths, graphs and charts that the pricing team use, and being able to explain what you're doing with a narrative structure rather than a technical structure can make a difference. Providing a narrative framework is important for two reasons: firstly, it proves you know what you're doing and that you're doing it for the right reasons; secondly, it helps others to understand and then accept the proposals you're making.

Particularly when it comes to how you do things in pricing, you'll be challenged by people who don't know the mathematics but do have important perspectives. You should listen to them because if you have concerns from people in your own organisation about how you're doing things, then once these get out into the wider world it's likely the concerns will be much worse. Often the concerns raised are about innocuous things, like particular buzzwords or a specific change they're not up to speed with.

Machine learning in particular has caused people a lot of concern because bias can often creep in. There is an attitude in some circles that mathematical functions cannot be biased, and this is true, they can't be; however, the data you put into them and how you operate them can be, and this is why you need to talk to other people who don't think like the pricing team.

The product committee

The product committee is made up of members from across the organisation and has a remit to manage the wider aspects of the product, such as the claims spend, customer service levels, marketing and many other aspects. It is not dedicated to pricing but pricing is one of its key responsibilities.

When proposals come to the product committee, it should be clear that the process set by the technical committee has been followed and the pricing committee is in agreement with the proposal. Thereby providing the product committee with assurance of good-quality work to the appropriate standards.

It is important to split the technical and pricing committees so there is strong consensus via the technical committee on how things are done before approaching the work, thereby limiting the risk of delay. This also avoids becoming bogged down in the details of what has been done in the pricing or product committees after the work has been completed. In smaller companies, the members of these committees may have significant crossover and may not have a strict hierarchy, but it is still important to split them to ensure a clear and clean demarcation of responsibilities. So, the technical committee agrees the methods and processes allowed, and the pricing committee demonstrates that they have been followed and there are good controls over what is deployed.

Higher-level governance

The next level is the senior level, or you might have an executive committee. Typically, this level of committee concerns strategic decisions. The monthly decisions, or fairly routine decisions about pricing, do not need to be considered at this level; it's about the wider future strategy of what you're hoping to achieve.

If you're deploying big changes or anything that's not currently on the expected plan, or if there are sensitive areas, you'll need to notify the executive committee and have the changes authorised at the senior level. Risk logs will lay down the areas that are considered to be sensitive; for example, how you treat customers that need additional support, your approach to avoiding discrimination, or any area where your regulator is taking an interventionist approach. Those are things that would need to be discussed and authorised at a more senior level. You may also occasionally be asked to present something to the board of the organisation or to departments outside of the typical governance structure, and you may at times be asked to respond to questions from a regulator. There are people outside of the direct governance structure who you'll need to work with; for example, it's usual to have an audit section and you'll also have your reserving area that will likely do regular reviews of your work.

Building good relationships is important, and so is having good external challenge. You need to work with all the different departments within the organisation and complete the actions they ask you to. You need to prioritise, listen and take feedback on board. It's better for everyone if you can build those good working relationships from the start. For example, if you end up with lots of audit problems and you don't do what the audit team ask you to do, then they'll take more interest in your area, which becomes more of an overhead for you. They're behaving in the right way, whereas you would be behaving in the wrong way.

Working with customers

The pricing team should always be involved in discussions about the customer experience. When customers write, email or phone the organisation because they are querying their price or they're concerned about what's happened, or in more serious cases when they have a complaint, the pricing team needs to be made aware of the issue.

There's an anecdote from Silicon Valley about it being common in startup companies, particularly coders and programmers, to have to deal directly with customers when they report bugs. The programmers respond quickly to eliminate the bugs because they don't want to deal with the complaints. You should have the same attitude in a pricing team. I don't necessarily mean for the pricing team to communicate directly with the customer, unless that is deemed beneficial, but I do mean for them to get involved with the customer service agents and sales people who are speaking to the customer.

When a customer service agent comes to you because a customer's unhappy with a price and they want you to explain how it has been calculated, it's easy to give them a basic response such as 'Oh, the system is complicated and we carefully calculate your price' etc. When somebody in the pricing team is answering that same customer, people suddenly put a great deal more effort into finding out the reason for the problem, with the result that the customer outcomes improve because the price has improved.

It's important to have smooth transitions in your prices so that they behave in sensible ways. Most customers will not move house in a particular year and most customers will not change vehicle in a particular year, but some will and some people's prices might have to be corrected because of mistakes, or there could be complaints which result in their prices having to be changed. What you don't want is for the prices to move in unexplainable ways, as I will discuss in the modelling chapter.

When a customer changes their address, for example, because it's been entered incorrectly in the system, it's sensible for their price not to move. If their price does move substantially, then that's a poor customer experience. It's a difficult thing to explain and it does leave customers wondering why the pricing works in that way.

Similarly, if a customer changes their vehicle to a fairly similar vehicle, you would expect their price not to move substantially, but it's not unusual that it might. Excesses and deductibles are a good example of when this could happen. The amounts customers pay are notoriously complicated to model because there are so many different dynamics at play. Generally, you will want the price to reduce as the excess increases. If a customer changes their vehicle and the price moves in a strange way, then that's a problem. Problems like this tend to have disappeared in the organisations that have the pricing team directly dealing with customer expressions of dissatisfaction.

TOP TIPS FOR DEALING WITH FEEDBACK

- **Get your pricing team involved with customer feedback** and you'll find that customer outcomes substantially improve. Monitoring feedback and involving customer expressions of dissatisfaction and complaints in the management information (MI) that you produce can also be effective.

- **Have a feedback loop** to establish whether there was anything in your previous deployment that negatively impacted on the way customers engage with the complaints area and whether you could do something about that next time. This is a fairly soft way to improve customer outcomes. Apply the Five Whys outlined in the deployment chapter.

Sometimes pricing teams can be removed from the customer-facing areas of the business and it's good to break those barriers down by training your pricing staff in the compliance and regulations that impact your area to create better outcomes for everyone.

Social concerns, higher inflation rates and more general questions being raised about insurance mean we're now seeing more intervention from regulators. Responsibility for these areas will need to be held by you and individuals within your team if you're serious about compliance and the customer experience. Training your staff in compliance and how regulations affect them is therefore becoming increasingly important. It's good practice to let your team know the key things they should be aware of in their role and designate someone in your team to have ultimate responsibility for your rates being compliant.

I'm anticipating that we'll see the emergence of a dedicated role to do with pricing compliance over the next few years. It's not unusual to see pricing assurance teams now, but having a separate, slightly removed team whose main role is to monitor the pricing to be sure that it's effective would be a positive move forward. This might not include only monitoring compliance but also monitoring financial targets, performance and customer outcomes. These often exist in one way or another but I expect to see them brought together and becoming more important.

Pricing and reputation

There are risks when it comes to setting your prices and it's good to consider these and add these to your risk log. There's a substantial reputational risk because the media is always critical of insurance companies. Many insurers have suffered from negative publicity because of how they set their prices.

There are also systemic financial risks and legal risks that you could be vulnerable to if your pricing is not properly considered. In some countries, regulation is statutory and any breach of that regulation can incur fines or even prosecution. Your team need to understand this.

EXERCISE: Pricing governance

1. List the different areas involved in your pricing governance and consider if this is the right mix.
2. Ask yourself whether you're getting effective external challenge and then discuss that with your direct reports.
3. Get your team involved in customer expressions of dissatisfaction.
4. Get some good external challenge in your technical committee. Make sure it applies challenge in the right places and try to avoid including people who just want to bang their own drum.
5. Keep a risk log and review it regularly to make sure it's a living, breathing document you work with.
6. Get your team reviewing each other's code.

Summary

You can now see why governance is so important in pricing and why it's critical to ensure that peer review, management checks and committees are in place. Peer reviews need to include a review of code and include processes for confirming the accuracy of work completed. Peer review of models is not enough, and many problems occur because of inadequate checking and reviews of code.

When putting in place your committee structure there should be a split between the technical committee, which decides on the appropriate processes, data and methods for creating prices, and the pricing committee which controls and determines the prices you actually set. The technical committee is where a lot of detail should be debated to ensure the use of appropriate methods and the creation of quality modelling and analysis that is compliant with regulations and your company's policies. The technical committee benefits from outside input on the technical detail, especially from people who are not directly part of the structure of the pricing department. The pricing committee takes the wider view of the company's whole objectives, needs and strategy in determining the prices it sets. It should be given the proof that the methods of the technical committee have been followed so it can be confident when it authorises changes in prices.

If the pricing team deals with customer expressions of dissatisfaction as part of their role, there is a high chance that customer outcomes will improve dramatically. It also results in improvements in the quality of the prices and a reduction in queries from stakeholders and other departments.

PART TWO
BUSINESS

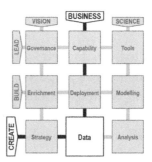

4
Data

Detailed data about the thing your company underwrites is one of your raw ingredients, and you will almost always need it to do any pricing. There are many approaches to data, but I have found that preprocessing it into a usable form is the most efficient way to ensure pricing activity is effective. In this chapter I'll explain the best way to achieve this.

How to structure pricing data

How do you get yourself to a position where you've got nice clean data that your analyst can work from?

The data that comes into the team is raw and it's not set up in the way your team or department will need it to be to do their work. When the available databases are not well prepared, work is done on an ad hoc basis and is often not reusable. It can be difficult to find out from your team whether the data is set up correctly, because those on the ground do not have the skills to assess this; they are simply working towards the next task and don't see the bigger picture.

To remedy this, you need to build structured data at the front end, and ideally you only want to do this once. Then you have to introduce processes that regularly update that data and make sure it's all accurate and correctly formatted so that whenever your analysts need to work they can just go straight to it. Of course, you'll need to update the database as you add new information or if the data changes, but once you have the process set up, it will be much easier to maintain.

There may be multiple versions of information within the same team, which can be frustrating, and often different departments or different teams can't even agree on basics like premium in a given time or earned exposure. When you have a standardised database of information which is correctly formatted and ready for analysis, you'll cut down a lot of the time your analysts spend doing data work, which means they can get on with setting prices. When everything is aligned between your teams, you can also use the data for your MI.

It's also worth remembering that the way data is held in databases like your Policy Administration System (PAS), your quotes data or your claims data is almost certainly not in a structure that's useful for doing analysis. It's common to store policy and quotes data in what's described as a 'horizontal' database, which usually has a huge number of rows in which each particular attribute gets its own line. Formatting the data in columns is much more conducive to doing analysis, but this is a different way of working and you might experience some frustration from your IT department and possibly even your data team.

Different people have different needs, and so when it comes to a database, it's easy to understand that people in other parts of the company might rather have data set out horizontally because they're only looking up the single or small number of items they need. If they want a particular field about a customer, then in the background the system can just go horizontally down that database, find that customer's record and that single attribute and fill in the particular box. That's a different need to yours. You're almost certainly never looking at just one item for one particular policyholder in isolation; you probably need to know the holistic view of exposure, and other attributes, for thousands of policyholders at the same time.

The best way to format your data

I've found the best way to format your policy data and your quotes data is to have it in rows for each quote or each policy and for each version of those. If a customer can request multiple quotes but they're all effectively part of the same attempt to buy a policy, then it's good to have an individual row for each time they've asked for a price, with all the different attributes held in the columns. You do similar with the policy, but you store each version of the policy so you then have a versions table of that policy where each row is a version and anything the customer changes about the policy during its lifetime gets a new row. For example, if they move address, you start a new row. If they make another change to the policy, it gets a new row. The start of the policy year is the start of a new row as well. You can happily use this set-up to analyse sales and retention development.

This is an efficient way to hold policy data when you're doing analysis, because if you want to know things like how much premium is generated by different rating factors, you just need to do a calculation by those rating factors of the premium and you've got the information you want. When you come to the claims tables, it's useful to have snapshots of the claims, so you have a row for each change in that claim as well. Claims data can often be a bit harder to manage because some claims systems will only hold the latest information about a claim, whereas often, in the background, snapshots have been taken for things like reserving. I suggest making rows for each version of a claim where you can't do that for each snapshot. Regular snapshots will also work. You'll end up with claims rows where there haven't been any changes

Policy ID	Version	Customer name	Coverage amount	Premium	Inception date	Policy start date	Policy end date	Version start date	Version end date
1	1	John Doe	100,000	500	1-Jan-23	1-Jan-23	31-Dec-23	1-Jan-23	15-Mar-23
1	2	John Doe	120,000	550	1-Jan-23	1-Jan-23	31-Dec-23	16-Mar-23	27-May-23
1	3	John Doe	123,000	560	1-Jan-23	1-Jan-23	31-Dec-23	28-May-23	8-Aug-23
1	4	John Doe	125,000	570	1-Jan-23	1-Jan-23	31-Dec-23	9-Aug-23	31-Dec-23
2	1	Sam Hill	145,000	670	1-Feb-23	1-Feb-23	31-Jan-24	1-Feb-23	15-Apr-23
2	2	Sam Hill	147,000	680	1-Feb-23	1-Feb-23	31-Jan-24	16-Apr-23	27-May-23
2	3	Sam Hill	150,000	690	1-Feb-23	1-Feb-23	31-Jan-24	28-May-23	31-Jan-24

A clean policy versions table

and rows where there have been multiple changes that haven't been recorded, but that's fine. If you then want to do analysis on claims development, you can happily attach your policy information to these claims rows.

If you want to then do something like a burning cost analysis, you only have to take the most recent versions of the claims and attach those to your policy data. To do a deep burning cost analysis, you'll need to turn the policy data into exposure data and the best way to do this is to use a calendar. A monthly calendar gives you a nice distinction between the seasonality of the year while not going into too much detail. Quarterly can work too for lines that aren't particularly sensitive to the weather. Once you add on this calendar file, most policies will end up having multiple rows, so you'll have many times more data than you started with. If there's a change in the year, you'll be adding on extra rows for that. This does make the data pool large, but it's the only real way to do a proper burning cost analysis. To the IT team and data engineers it can seem odd to work in this way, but it is what you need to analyse claims properly.

Overcoming problems caused by dates

Within your policy data you'll have dates, and dates are often what cause the most difficulties. You'll have a start date and an end date for the policy. You'll probably also have the date the policy was transacted on, and you might have a separate quote date. When analysing burning costs, you want to record the dates your exposure changes, because that's what a pricing exercise needs to be about.

The start date of the policy (the date it went on risk) and the end date of the policy (when it went off risk) are your anchor dates to work from. Obviously, your data will have its own nuances and it's good to get these properly recorded and documented so they're not just circulated by word of mouth. A typical example of this might be that agents, or indeed the customer online, can change the start dates and the end dates of the policy, which then makes for some complicated transactions.

Your system might not be the best at recording whether the policy had gone on risk or not before the start and end date were changed, so it's good to get decent documentation on this. If it doesn't exist in the organisation, it's down to you to put it together and that's another reason why it's advisable to clean and format this data centrally rather than leaving it up to different analysts.

Claims and exposure data

You also have the version dates of your policy, and it's important to clean these so that your versions run chronologically. There's no point having multiple versions on the same day; however, if your data does record the times that changes are made, then the best way to do this is to have multiple versions with time-stamps. If your data doesn't record the timestamps, then a maximum of one version a day is probably what you have to work with.

Once you've got your versions for each policy and they're running chronologically, and you've got clean dates about when the policy started and ended, you want to have one record for each exposure period when the policy's on risk. This means that when you do your analysis, you can understand things like how time is affecting the risk. This is particularly important when there's a high-inflation environment and also when you're dealing with seasonal lines of business.

Once you've turned your policy data into those lines, you're going to want to attach your claims to it. It's important that you end up with your claims in the right exposure period so that you can build your risk premium. This is straightforward, but people often make a mess of it. You need to attach the policies to the claims to find out which policy version and expo-sure period goes with each claim, and then you want to enter the exposure month that starts and ends with the claim in between it so it's held with your claims data. Once you've got that indexed, you can calcu-late the cost of the claims and the counts of the claims and then attach that back to the exposure data. There is a variation of this where the version ends at the claim – that is fine if you especially want to only ever have one claim per version.

This is how you end up with a nice clean table and have all your claims in the right places and all your policies with the right exposure information. You can now use that for any analysis or MI you need to produce. The bottom-line advice here is to only build this once. Don't have your analyst build it every time they want to do some work, as that's inefficient. Build it once, store it centrally and update it regularly, ideally on a daily basis, but if not then weekly or, at worst, monthly.

Quotes data

Quotes data is different from your exposure and claims data. It's common for there to be multiple versions of a quote, and if you try doing your analysis with multiple versions, you'll often end up with lots of lines of data, a low response rate and many quotes that customers didn't intend to buy from. It's normal to have duplicate quotes with slight variations, but when you come to deduplicate quotes, however you do it in your analytical environment, you need to be able to reproduce that in your impact analysis and, if you're doing any form of live optimisation, in your live environment.

Taking either the last quote that a customer made or the quote they purchased is a fairly common way of deduplicating quotes. There's no great reason to favour one method over another; consistency is what matters.

Matching the pricing data with the finance data

The price ledger is a set of the tables I've talked about in the sections above. It consists of:

- Your nicely cleaned policy versions table
- Your snapshot claims versions table
- Your quotes data

It's important to be able to match your data to your finance team's numbers. The financial analysis is different to a pricing analysis, and the way things are measured on your accounting basis is going to be different to how you measure them on the underwriting or accident basis.

To do this, you start off with your totals and, until you're sure that your totals are correct, you shouldn't attempt to match things like monthly differences. It shouldn't be too difficult to get your totals lined up; if there are differences, you need to talk them through with both departments to understand the reason for those differences. Often complications arise from things like charges or add-ons; for example, you might consider something like a protected no-claims discount to be a core part of the cover, whereas the finance team might consider it an add-on.

It's easy to get frustrated at this point because the pricing team may feel that their data is correct and if it doesn't line up with the finance data that's because finance are wrong. Generally, finance are not wrong, they just have a different way of measuring these things. They hold the data that most people in the organisation will believe to be correct, they provide figures to regulators and tax authorities, and theirs is the true and fair view; it just might not be structured and presented in the same way as you need for pricing.

It's the responsibility of the pricing department to ensure that their numbers match up with those of finance. To grasp any differences and where they come from, you need to understand how the finance team measure things and how you're measuring the same things. Waterfall charts are a good way to see those differences visually.

Updating the data

If you're able to, it's best to build out some part of your department that's dedicated to keeping this data current, flowing and clean. If you fill it with people who have the right skill sets to do that, those people will then also become responsible for updates to the data. Things will naturally shift over time as you change the questions you're asking or the third parties you work with, or when there are systems changes. You'll need to have a change function so that you can amend the data as you go forward.

You need to make sure you have robust processes that reduce the need for manual intervention, especially with things like policy reconciliation, which you can run after you've made changes to the data. To remain confident that your data's in line with finance and the other parts of the organisation, you could also ask your team to produce regular reports, making sure they are read and checked and that there is feedback when things aren't right.

Where you're adding in a new set of external data, for example, your analyst will have worked on that data – they are likely to have cleaned it and attached it to their policy data when they did their analysis. It's a good idea at that point to involve the pricing team and the people who did the analysis when building that data. Proper logic and documentation should be produced, checked and tested.

Your analytical team will have made changes to the data and cleaned it, or made assumptions when they used that data to test it out. If you don't check and test the data, the changes made by the analytical team may not be repeated when it's built into the system, so you end up with differences between live and analytical. For example, the analytical team might have used a particular version of the data that came out in a particular month, and then time rolls forward so the data team use another version. You can see straight away that you'll end up with a difference, and you can begin to understand why it's so important to make sure you are all working from the same versions of the data.

If you want to have the latest versions of some external data but also be able to reproduce previous analyses, then you'll have to maintain multiple versions of a piece of external data, which can become difficult and lead to mistakes. Keeping quality logs up to date can mitigate these issues.

A lot of these problems come down to miscommunication, or noncommunication, between teams. It's easy to make mistakes, but the issue is not so much the mistake as the absence of good processes in place for checking the work and signing it off. Rather than point to someone on the ground and say 'You should have coded this properly', in reality the question should be 'Why isn't there a system in place that checks this properly?'

You don't want to just find the surface problems; you need to get to the root cause of why mistakes occur. It might be that the data analyst built the data differently from the way the pricing team did; maybe the specification from the pricing team wasn't clear, or maybe the pricing team didn't realise they needed to make the specification clear enough for the data team to build it exactly. In each case, you should look at why the error happened. Every mistake has a cause, and tracing this cause back to its origin will enable you to avoid making the same mistake again.

You need a good specification, you need a good way of checking that the specification is correct, and then you need to be able to reproduce your previous analysis to check not only whether the change has been made correctly but also that it's not broken anything else in the data or the systems. It's just about making sure you've got all your ducks in a row before you start going down the wrong pathway.

Generally, if you do make mistakes in the data space, it's quite easy to come back from them with little cost attached. If there is an error, it will be found and then it's a simple matter of making a change, although of course it's preferable it doesn't happen in the first place.

You might have produced analyses that are incorrect, which can be embarrassing, but it doesn't usually cost the company money. When you get to the deployment chapter, you'll see there are pathways you can go down that are difficult to come back from if you don't make the right call, and which can cost the company a lot of money to rectify. It's worth noting that if you get things right in your analytical space and your data space, then you should naturally get them right in your deployment space.

TOP TIPS FOR MANAGING DATA

- Allow the pricing team to be in control of its own data.
- Preprocess centrally in pricing to create the pricing ledger and use this for all your needs.
- Work with as much raw data as possible.
- Avoid situations where your team have to go to the raw data and set things up again.
- Include repeated tasks in the central data production.
- Ensure there is a feedback loop for the team to make changes.
- Give the data team responsibility for correctly implementing changes from the rest of the team, and make sure the rest of the team provide accurate logic and instructions to the data team.
- Task the pricing teams with creating a good set of examples for the data team to use for checking – often this should be data created during the pricing teams' analysis.

Summary

In this chapter I've explained how to structure policy claims and quotes data into a pricing ledger and why it's so important to get this framework in place to avoid data errors. I have also shown the best ways to structure data to ensure your team is able to efficiently complete work without losing precious time and resources having to repeatedly set up data themselves on an ad hoc basis.

I have given you tips for reconciling your data to the finance team and explained why they are generally right and so why it is your responsibility to match them or at least understand any material differences other than those caused by the different basis used for analysing and presenting the information. You and your team need to be able to show your data matches to finance and you need to be able to demonstrate the reasons and magnitude of differences.

Dates often cause particular issues. It is important to ensure a clean chronological flow of the transactions in policy, quote and claims data. This shows the data is consistent and correct, meaning it can be used for our purposes with confidence that we are producing good output. So much of insurance is about the response to the circumstances. Be it the happening of a claim or the choice to buy or not to buy. These are responses to the circumstances as they are at a particular point in time. Having good records of each point in time is essential.

You should put in place automatic processes to update data and recreate comparisons so you and the company can be confident that pricing is well run and in control. It's also important for teams to work together to ensure that data is clean and consistent across departments.

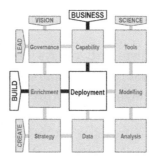

5
Deployment

W hat you do is only as good as what you deploy. You have to get all that you do in pricing out into the real world before it can make a noticeable difference to customers and the business, and the way you do that is at the heart of the nine-step method. In this chapter I'll discuss the pricing architecture and explain why it's important to be able to forecast and communicate how price changes impact on the business and your customers.

How do you get your prices out into the world?

There are several types of pricing architecture. The most common two are bespoke and built in-house, and bought off the shelf.

There are two ways this architecture is used. Historically, insurance companies handed responsibility for the pricing architecture to the IT department who would structure the rating and handle the testing and deployment. At this point, any problems became the responsibility of that department even though the pricing team may still have to get deeply involved to achieve the deployment, and there are still some instances where IT will manage the coding end of the prices and the deployment.

This is an inflexible way of working and not necessarily the most productive: it can cause frustrations to many concerned, and blurred responsibilities are rarely efficient. IT may structure things in a way that is sensible for now, but without the knowledge of pricing and the complicated mathematics involved, changes become Byzantine. If you want to make changes, you need to discuss this with IT, and if they have to make changes it can be costly and take a lot of time, as those changes are considered against IT's other priorities. Specifying the requirements of a pricing algorithm that allows for fast changes to nonlinear calculations and optimisation routines to those not trained in pricing mathematics is a recipe for confusion and a wasted effort. While I am sure IT teams are not biased in their assessments, I am also sure that it will take someone who is trained in pricing much less time to design and build a pricing algorithm than someone who is not, the latter leading to high estimates for the IT work and build involved. It reminds me of the film *Armageddon* where the American space agency teaches miners to be astronauts. It would have made more sense to teach the existing astronauts how to operate the drill.

That way of doing things is ending now and all insurance teams, not just the pricing teams, are becoming multidisciplinary in their approach. There is a shift towards moving these functions into pricing with the help of flexible pricing systems. The trend is for pricing teams to manage systems and deployment for themselves, but this often includes having to manage quite complicated IT deployment processes on top of a team's regular work. It's becoming more important for pricing teams to future-proof their departments because in the future more and more of the IT-related processes will be managed by the pricing team.

There are a range of off-the-shelf IT systems that the pricing teams can use, and they vary in their approach – see the tools chapter for more information about this. The current trend is towards on-rail systems which teams have the flexibility to customise: this is how you get your prices out into the world. There is good new generation software that also gives you a lot of control over what's being deployed, and you could potentially have a control panel where you can see different versions of the rate, what's currently live, and where you can schedule new rates on particular dates. Gone are the days when someone has to stay up until 11.00pm to push 'go' on a new set of prices.

How do you calibrate prices?

Ultimately what is in the raw risk premium is just a reflection of the data, it's not the real world. It's often the case that people put too much stock in the models and think of them as being the absolute view of the world, but sadly they're not.

We have to use our knowledge and collect all the information we can. We have to listen and read reports then make decisions about what we put into our rates to allow for externalities like inflation. It's important to be flexible with this, especially in a high-inflation environment, and it's entirely possible for claims inflation to be high even in periods when the general economic inflation is low. If you happen to have periods of high litigation that can drive up your costs, even though the general inflation in the economy might be relatively low, this will also impact on your pricing. You also need to make adjustments for catastrophes and large losses, and this can be complicated. You can use catastrophe models and you can get data, information and suggestions from other organisations – reinsurers can be helpful to you in this regard.

Ultimately insurance exists to protect people from losses. In some jurisdictions you may have almost unlimited liabilities to pay out for accidents or incidents, and these are the hard things to predict. You never have enough data at that end, but you know that you have to put money aside for those claims. Again, the use of reinsurers and talking about your loans with other organisations can be helpful with this. Other calibrations, like underwriting adjustments, involve making alterations that are often outside of your data and raw risk premium and that are based on your or someone else's knowledge and experience. You must ensure you act with deep knowledge of what you are insuring.

You may change covers, or the external legal environment around you might change, or it might be there are places where your exposure is low. You could be launching something new where there is no data, there may be distortions and correlations in your data, or you might see factors that give certain levels to your rates but which you know are distorted. For these types of case, you need to make some adjustments. This is the key reason why humans beat the machines: we have that wider knowledge of what we are insuring.

How do you prevent errors?

So many things can go wrong when you try to deploy your prices. Previously, I've talked about the importance of consistency between your live environments and your

PRICE WRITER

analytical environments, and to achieve this you need to try to align your mappings. You should map everything to fully understand what's going on and you should have quality documentation that people can readily access and use to make sure these mappings are correct.

Get your end prices accurate

Here is a hypothetical example related to external lookups for the attributes of customers' cars. One of these elements could be the weight of the car. Knowing how heavy a car is may affect the burning cost because you might expect a heavier car to be likely to cause more damage. One day, while analysing the back-end data, an analyst might spot that in the live environment there are a lot of light vehicles that hadn't been there when they looked at the analytical data. They might go on to discover the vehicle weight attribute was expected to be in kilograms but a lot of the vehicles were being given measurements that would have made them micro-machines. The live data stated that a car was, for example, 1.5 kilograms and the analyst would realise that when the car's measurements had been requested by the live system the string that was returned would usually be in kilograms but sometimes in metric tonnes. The measurement field that indicated whether the data was in kilograms or tonnes was being completely ignored. As a result, customers were given lower insurance quotes and this would be likely to cost the company significant sums of money. There are lots of inherent

94

problems like this within data because issues like these may not have been eliminated.

Print the correct information

You can run into problems with other fields that are returned by your rating engine. Some of the information is printed on customer documents but may not impact on what is charged. In theory an insurer could incorrectly calculate some of the numbers that go onto the customer documentation. Because they don't affect the customer's end price it might not be spotted. It might not be included in the testing. This links to what I covered in the chapter on governance, but if no one in the organisation has ownership of all the numbers returned, even those not directly charging the customer, then there could be a problem.

We have all heard other stories like the urban legend of an insurer printing the customer's policy number, which is several digits long, incorrectly in the customer's price section. It would probably be swiftly noticed but customers could receive renewal letters that quote the cost as being many millions of pounds because the reference number had been printed in the wrong field.

Check the numbers carefully

It's difficult to completely prevent errors from happening because the systems are complicated and you don't always know there's a problem until it's found;

however, through good testing procedures it should be possible to eliminate many of those that result in errors going live. A good first step is to ensure someone has clear responsibility for all of the figures returned by the rating engine.

Your first real line of defence is to check the numbers carefully. You'll want to run a good-sized batch of either test data or real quotes through your system and then look at the results. Usually, it's best to have some automation to help with this, but you can have it done manually. The difficulty with doing it manually is that it's the sort of task that people end up not paying enough attention to.

If you look at lots of sets of numbers over and over again, you start to understand what's going on with them and that's why it's good to have system checks in place. With the issue of printing the wrong numbers on the letters, a simple system check – 'Are any of these numbers bigger than the premium, yes or no?' – would have highlighted the problem. Making sure you're running the data through a test version of the live environment is also important because things will naturally change when they go live.

You should also check the renewals and look at how prices have changed between what the customer's currently paying to what you're expecting to renew at. You've almost certainly got some logic in your system and you might have regulatory rules you need to follow. You might have to keep your new business and your renewal prices the same, or you might be expecting your new business prices to rise by whatever you've set as your cap. When you do a system check, you'll be able to see whether any of these items fall outside of those rules, and if so you'll need to investigate why that's happening.

You should also introduce a regression check between your previous set of rates and your new set of rates. You should have an idea of the changes you're making to your prices and set rules and tolerances to flag issues. For example, if you're making an inflationary increase in the rates, you'll want to flag anything that changes in an unexpected way. You'll also need to make sure you segment your test results and check the subsections of the data too.

When you run the tests, you should use consistent batches and a good-sized sample – somewhere in the region of a million quotes or a hundred thousand renewals would be reasonable numbers to use. Using real policies and quotes is best but generated ones can be effective too. It's important to make sure that someone in your team takes responsibility for these checks because the pricing team will be held accountable for any problems that might occur. It may be that you're not to blame and the issue is caused by IT or other departments, but as you're responsible for the pricing, the company will look to you for solutions.

The Five Whys

The Five Whys is a strategy developed by Toyota to deal with problems that happened on their production lines. You can use this method to ask yourself why something went wrong. For example, if you've deployed something with errors, if your impact analysis hasn't held up, or if you haven't been able to communicate the data effectively, you can use this method to understand what went wrong and why.

I'll use the fictional example above where the wrong numbers were printed on the customer letters to explain the method.

1. **Why did that happen?** The first answer you get is because something was coded wrongly in the system, but that doesn't help you to understand the whole issue or prevent it from occurring again.

2. **It is difficult to expect analysts to code everything correctly first time so why wasn't this error found in the testing or review?** The answer to that might be 'Because we don't review the code and we only run tests on fields that directly impact on the end price charged to the customer.'

3. **Why do we only check and test fields that do impact on the end customer price?** The answer might be because no one has responsibility for

making sure the items printed on the customer communications are correct unless they directly affect what the customer pays.

4. **Why don't we have someone who is responsible for the accuracy and correctness of these fields?** The answer would be that it has not been considered in the past to be an area that would impact on the success of the prices.

5. **Why has it not been considered in the past to be an area that would impact on the success of the prices?** The final answer is that the governance of the business does not consider ownership of these items, and so there is no clear objective for these to be correct.

By working this through, we have gone from the sticking plaster answer of 'an analyst made a mistake' to the root of the issue. The root cause is that the governance and objective need to be updated, although it doesn't stop there – we also uncovered potential needs for better training and reviews of code.

How do you communicate the impact of changes?

You can use your test batches again and run them against both your previous sets and your new sets of rates to check they behave in the way you expect. This gives you a good start for your impact analysis.

You've built algorithms to understand demand and price elasticity, and now you can run those through the system to see and understand the potential impacts of your price changes.

It's good to know how skilled you are at forecasting these things, and people don't go back and do this enough. You need to know whether the forecasting you've done in the past gave the results you expected or were far off. This is not about pointing the finger but about learning and getting better at forecasting. You can then feed that information back into the system. Ultimately you want to be able to reach a conclusion about high-level pricing changes and the impact this will have. For example, 'We expect X per cent change in the premium that we collect or the amount of conversions we get.'

You then need to understand how this impacts on individual customers and how it will change customer outcomes. It's a good idea to look at future predictions if your system allows you to do this. You don't want to know just what the predicted impact is for the current year but also how it might affect year two and year three. For example, you'll want to have an idea of how many customers are likely to stay with you for a certain period.

Communicating price changes can be difficult because you're used to working with hundreds of thousands of lines of data; however, the question that matters is 'How does this affect a customer?' This approach involves a different mindset because you might well be quoting the average impact, but the company will be genuinely thinking of a person who receives their renewal and what that looks like for them.

Communicating the range of outcomes with other stakeholders and teams can be difficult. The best approach is to use a mixture of narrative-based descriptions with some charts. Explaining that some customers will see X whereas other customers will see Y is a much easier way for people to understand how changes will impact different types of customer. Explaining this by using a scenario with commentary rather than using only numerical values, which can be off-putting for some, can help bring people with you.

EXERCISE: The Five Whys

1. What's the most recent error you've encountered?
2. Apply the Five Whys to the problem to determine the root cause.
3. What can you do to ensure that it doesn't happen again?

Summary

Deployment is the act of getting all the good pricing work out into the world, and getting it right is essential to achieving your objectives and targets. Successful deploys demonstrate very publicly that you are running your team well. Getting deployment wrong ruins all of the rest of the good work. Everything else is for nothing if deployment goes wrong. This is the part that really matters because it is the way you are in contact with customers.

We need to calibrate prices to allow for the ever-changing world and for the information that is not directly in your pricing data. Calibration aligns the reflection of the real world that you have created with your mathematical methods and analysis with how the future will really be. It is one of the most crucial steps in having good prices. It is not a tick box exercise and is as important as anything else you and your team do.

I have shown how and why you should put in processes and systems that reduce the possibility of errors in the deployed prices. This checking and testing should be treated with the same level of rigour that changes to a crucial IT system would be. Pricing defects, problems or errors can be serious issues. Not just in customer impact, but in demonstrating inadequate or poor controls and procedures. I have shown some hypothetical examples of what can go wrong. You can see why deployment is so important and why it's essential to complete regular system and data checks to ensure that there are no errors.

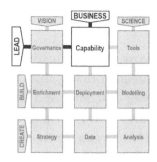

6
Capability

I n this chapter we'll consider the organisation and resourcing of the modern pricing team and how these impact on the success of your organisation.

The modern pricing team is like a finely tuned orchestra. There are many sections, many instruments and lots of different people who have different functions and specialise in different things, but they all follow the same rhythm and work in harmony towards the same outcome, and everyone has the same goal.

Just as with an orchestra, one small mistake will ruin the whole performance. If one person stops or a string breaks somewhere, then it means disaster for everyone. In a pricing team, even a minor error could ruin the whole price strategy and undo a lot of the good work you've already done. In the minds of the people outside pricing, this one small mistake could result in poor outcomes and unhappy customers, and unfortunately this error might end up being what the pricing team is remembered for.

It's therefore important to remember that, just as with an orchestra, your pricing team needs to rehearse before going live. Your rehearsal will be the testing, checking and refining you'll need to do to identify and iron out any flaws in the pricing system. You need to make sure that your team will perform flawlessly because flaws in your rates can add up to a lot of problems, lead to a lot of complaints, and potentially result in large amounts of money being lost. When you go live, you're on a stage for all to see. You need to understand that the customer and your stakeholders are your audience, and you don't want them to see anything that's not perfect.

The pricing team does not work in isolation and it's important to remember that the work you're doing isn't just building esoteric mathematical systems for the fun of it; you're working with real customers' prices and people will decide whether or not to buy a product from you based on what those prices are. Customers will arrange their annual household budgets around their insurance costs, and so of course they are going to weigh up carefully which products they purchase and which insurers they buy from.

When it's you who's in front of the customer and when you also have a responsibility to the many stakeholders in the organisation, you can see why it's so important to get it right. If we go back to the orchestra analogy, all the people whose jobs rely on the orchestral performances – the people who work the venues, the box office team – need to know that the orchestra is going to turn up and put on a good show. In insurance, everyone in the company is reliant on the pricing team delivering what they need to and performing well as a team.

How do you structure a pricing team?

The two most common ways to structure a pricing team are to orientate your team either around the products and channels you have or around a function.

Structuring around the product

The number of sub-teams you have will depend on how many product lines you do. It's not unusual to see a fairly sizeable team for the largest product and a slightly smaller one for the next product in line. At some point the projects will be lumped together and will end up in a miscellaneous area, and some might be split between people who work on commercial products and those who work on personal products.

The problem with structuring the pricing team in this way is that often you'll find that people will migrate into areas based on their interest in a particular product. This means that all too often you'll end up with your best people on the biggest product, because unsurprisingly it's the one that gets the most attention from the rest of the organisation and people will know that being on this product means a fast track to promotion and an easy way to raise their profile.

Your next set of people will be working on your second-best product and these are also often skilled people; however, this approach doesn't work well because your biggest product might not be the one you can have the biggest impact on or the one that's your most profitable. This means that this way of orientating your team is both ineffective and a poor way to develop your staff, who will end up becoming specialists in one product, resulting in your department's capabilities becoming concentrated. Your opportunities to do clever things with your pricing might be presented by your smaller products where you can get an advantage and grow the business, but if your best people are not working on these types of product, this is a missed opportunity.

When you organise your department around the product like this, the barrier to movement is high because people won't want to move away from the biggest product to a smaller one; they will want to migrate in the direction that is perceived as upwards.

Structuring around a function

The second most common way of organising a pricing team is around a function. Imagine teams working in a chain. The first team will create your data and your pricing ledgers. This is then passed to a second team, your risk premium modelling team, who might also work on demand modelling. You'll then have a third team who work on the street pricing.

There are variations in how you organise this and you might also have a team that's specifically working on risk premiums, but teams that are structured around a function will undertake tasks like working out what the company's large claims loading and expenses should be.

The street pricing team will then work out what the final price for the customer is, allowing for the adjustments that need to be made for different lines and channels of business etc. This team will take into account the different ways the customer might come to you, and it will also deal with the complexities of running a business and having customers with the business for different lengths of time. Often you'll have different sets of information for different cohorts of customers, so the street pricing team will deal with a lot of complexities but will always try to find the right final price for customers which meets the company's objectives. The process will then move on to the deployment team who aim to get the built prices out into the world. This will require IT deployment, testing and governance.

The problem with working in this way as functions in a line is that to some extent the importance of the product is forgotten in the process, and you might well find the entire chain works only on the biggest products or that too much time is being given to the smaller products.

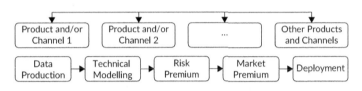

The two most common ways of structuring a Pricing Department

Hybrid ways of working

Another approach I've seen work well in organisations is when a hybrid way of working is adopted. This approach requires teams to be orientated so that they work in chains. You'll have data, modelling, street and deployment teams, but you'll also have people within the larger team who are focused on a particular product. It's this team's responsibility to make sure their own product gets the resources necessary to drive it through and that their own projects are completed. This team will also be ultimately responsible for delivering the results.

There might also be performance people in these product teams who will be monitoring the MI and making sure that the products are delivered well. Each product team might also have business partners – people who also work with other teams such as finance, underwriting and claims – and they will take the lead and liaise between their specialist team and the product teams to ensure that everything works holistically.

It's also a good idea to have people who are experts on the particular product or item that is being insured. For example, you will generally find people in a pricing team who are excited about cars, or properties, or liability. Try to harness this interest and use it to the organisation's advantage.

You need to have people who are organisers and managers within your teams. There should be a leader, or a project manager, in each area and they should be focused on delivering a particular project and making things work in concert. Having someone who drives that work through and ensures that it's delivered on time is key to achieving outcomes, and the most effective way of designing a modern team.

The right resources

The resources you need are often dictated by the structure described above. One of the reasons why the hybrid model works so well is because it gives balance to the organisation. Some pricing teams can be full of people who are just there for the academic side of things: they're interested in building mathematical models, but they're not so focused on the reality that they are working on real people's prices and so have to get them deployed correctly. You sometimes see a sudden and absolute focus on accuracy when it comes to modelling, but that often disappears when you get to the deployment stage, which is disappointing.

It's common for pricing to attract analytically minded and process-orientated people, and it's good to have a balance of both. It's also good to have people who can manage and lead, and people who can see the bigger picture, especially as teams are getting larger and larger. People who can manage teams and departments are in demand and section leaders, team leaders and people who can get the best out of the people working for them are valuable to the organisation.

This is because for some people the interest is in building the models. Sometimes even the most ambitious people only want to produce the prices, and so they step away from leadership roles. The people who are ambitious and good at management usually end up running large departments because that's what the organisation needs, but this means that the organisation can end up with an empty area in between (the management area), which is difficult to recruit people for. People either want to push upwards out of this area as fast as possible or have no real ambition in taking on the role at all.

A way to get around this, and something I've seen work well in some organisations, is to have what we would call 'lead contributors'. People are given the prestige and position you would expect a manager to receive, but they are leading in a technical sense, they're not necessarily running an actual team. We often expect managers to facilitate and deliver training on top of their usual technical and managerial responsibilities. Lead contributors are frequently good at teaching and training and so they can fulfil a lot of the duties that managers have, reducing the pressure on managers and saving them time.

I've seen this done well and it's an approach that is becoming more and more respected. I've also seen it done in theory but not in practice, and of course this is going to be much less effective. The problem is that if you don't offer people the opportunity to contribute, they will probably leave the organisation and will almost certainly start freelancing or contracting, where they will be paid much larger amounts of money for doing the technical-level work because that's the work they enjoy doing, and your organisation loses that experience. If you can foster people's interests, use their skills and give them the opportunity to grow and develop without pushing them into management, your organisation will reap the rewards.

Specialists versus generalists

Studies have shown that specialists often perform worse, even in the thing they specialise in, than people with wider, more generalised skills, but this can go unnoticed because when people have such huge knowledge about their specialism, their lower levels of productivity can be missed.[4]

The way to avoid this is by not putting people in a position where they're doing repeated tasks over and over again, even if that's their preference. You want to keep people happy, of course, but if they're not developing then they're usually getting worse at what they're doing because they don't have the ability to see the bigger picture.

You need to develop people so they have broad skill sets and avoid becoming deeply specialised in one aspect of the process. Having specialists within the organisation is also inefficient from a people management perspective because if you've got many focused specialists it becomes hard for them to work together as a team, to understand the struggles and the difficulties other areas are having, and to then pull together when it's needed.

---

4   D Epstein, *Range: Why generalists triumph in a specialized world* (Riverhead Books, 2021)

The importance of good subject knowledge

It's important to know about what you're insuring, ie what you're setting the prices on. If you work in underwriting or in claims, for example, you can study particular aspects of the process and become certified in them via widely recognised qualifications, but sadly we don't have that available to us in GI. It's difficult to get people trained and externally certified in insurance pricing, although the training that I've developed goes some way to addressing this.

Teaching people about the thing they're insuring sounds simple, but it can be surprisingly effective. Without training, people often draw lines between spurious things in the data that aren't necessarily meaningful and can be hard to explain. They might also miss important details that they wouldn't if they knew more about what was being insured. For example, if people knew more about the legal side of liability insurance, they would be better able to do their work.

It's also important to develop people's skills and provide them with training in different computing and programming languages. It's often the case that data science courses are focused on the sort of problems you might have if you worked for a technology company, but these problems are different from the work that we do in pricing. This is why you need to ensure you offer your people useful training that is relevant to their work.

You also need to train people in deployment and how to forecast the future, manage performance and analyse data. These are all individual skills that you can't just send someone on a generalist training course to learn. We often expect our managers (who are already extremely busy) to provide the training in all of these areas, and of course the reality is that the training doesn't happen or it's delivered ineffectively.

Staff need to be trained in compliance because in most countries the regulators are becoming more and more interested in pricing. They want to see both that customers are treated fairly and that the organisation's customer service matches up with regulations and legislation on issues like equality and diversity. The regulators will also want reassurance that the most vulnerable in society are not paying unfairly high premiums to subsidise those who are in better circumstances. Unfortunately, you can't send people on a general compliance course and have them learn only about GI pricing. You need to give them options about pricing because more and more people's jobs touch on legal and compliance issues and it's hard to navigate those without good training.

Engaging with people inside and outside of pricing

Pricing is a hot area in a lot of organisations and it's usually a sizeable department within the firm. Many years ago, there were maybe two or three people in a pricing team. Now, for a large insurer, it's not unusual for there to be hundreds, and departments are continuing to grow. It's not unlikely that soon pricing teams will rival claims teams in the number of members they have. You therefore expect the pricing department to have the same level of engagement as you'd expect from the claims or finance departments.

You might want to think about whether you require things like business partners – people from the pricing team who are designated to work with other teams. This can be an effective way of making sure the organisation works well as a whole. Being involved in strategic communications and internal communications can also be helpful. You might even consider putting out regular communications – a brief note from the pricing leader to the department once a week or month can help with team cohesion. Other regular communications are also beneficial to everyone, such as connecting with the rest of the business once or twice a year to introduce the kind of things the pricing team are working on and ask for feedback from other areas within the organisation.

It's all about building trust within the organisation and understanding where other departments are coming from. It's not uncommon for the organisation to feel disconnected from the pricing team because what we do is so technical and not an area other people know or understand. However, like a flywheel or a snowball, the effort you put into building those relationships and speaking to other departments builds your knowledge and fosters trust in you and your department. It's always the case that the more you put into the process, the more you get out of it and, over time, the better skilled you become.

Nowadays, it's even more important for people across the organisation to have that trust and understanding in what you do because insurance is becoming more and more regulated. If you show up consistently and are open and honest about what you do, people who may have doubts about the impact of pricing, for example, or about your ability to meet regulatory requirements, will feel more confident.

Ultimately what you want is for your biggest advocates to be the people who work inside your organisation. What you don't want is for people to feel that pricing is a black box. People often talk about this concept of black boxes and how they don't want to use systems and processes they don't fully understand. Imagine how you're seen by other departments within the organisation – you want to avoid being viewed as a black box yourselves. You don't want to have a situation whereby the rest of the organisation doesn't understand or appreciate the work you do.

EXERCISE: Mapping your team

1. Look at the structure of your team and your department and consider whether it's got a good balance of skills. The skills you'll need are:

   - Data engineering
   - Data science
   - Analytics
   - Deployment
   - Training
   - Communications

2. Do you have a good balance of responsibilities in your team? These include business partners, organisers and managers, and subject matter experts and performance leaders who can make sure you stay on target for meeting the financial needs of the organisation as well as the customer outcomes.

3. If the answer is no for questions 1 and 2, where do you feel you are over- or under-represented?

4. How many people were in your team when you started? How many people do you work with now? How many people do you think you'll have in your team in ten years' time?

Summary

You can see that deciding how to structure your pricing team is an important consideration. Getting the right people working in the right places and making sure they have the right skills is key to the success of the pricing department. I have shown the two most common ways of broadly structuring a pricing team and demonstrated how I think a hybrid approach, that takes on elements of the two, is the best approach. Structuring around products and channels has the downside of concentrating resource on the largest, most prestigious products. Structuring around functions has the downside of not being able to easily control the resource given to the products and channels. A hybrid overcomes these issues and allows for greater movement around the team.

Pricing naturally attracts logical and mathematical thinkers, with analytical and process skills being very common but it is important to have diversity of thought and ability. Management skills are especially in demand. People that understand pricing and can organise teams and deliver against plans and goals are in short supply. I have shown evidence of why it is important to work with and employ generalists who have multiple skills and knowledge. You should avoid you or your team becoming specialists because this diminishes the productivity and overall ability of you and your team.

Pricing teams are growing quickly and are becoming some of the largest functions in companies. You need to ensure you and your department have the skills to manage both the team size, and the growth, effectively and efficiently. Some people underestimate the value of management, but it is a powerful and necessary skill.

PART THREE
SCIENCE

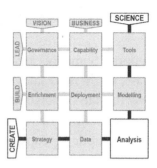

7
Analysis

I n this chapter I'll explain why correct analysis is so important and what reports to turn your data into. Although often overshadowed by modelling, analysis is an important area in its own right. Good analysis can drive you forward in a faster time frame and allow you to understand and adapt to the circumstances and environment. It puts you in a position of power to control your prices and allows you to communicate the good work you do in facts and figures, but only if you get the information right.

Management information reports

Everyone knows you need MI, but what is the minimum you need to run an effective pricing department? I say you need daily, weekly, monthly, quarterly and annual reports. Someone accessing the MI report on a daily basis might need sales figures for the last day or the past few days to understand performance. People looking at it on a monthly or weekly basis might be analysing run rates to update people in meetings about the state of the business and to decide on short-term action. If the MI is accessed on an annual or quarterly basis, that would usually be for a governance function such as in a committee.

You need to be able to review sales and claims information on at least an accident basis and an underwriting basis and it is also sensible to have the sales and accounting basis too. This means that the data is turned regularly into available reports of:

- Policy counts
- Premium – net and gross of commissions and reinsurance
- Loss ratio – net and gross of commissions and reinsurance
- Claims frequency, severity and burning cost
- Sales development
- Claims development
- Conversion and retention rates
- Expected loss ratios based on your risk premiums
- Market prices (where available)
- Benchmarking (where available)

You will need all of this information for all of your rating factors and other important dimensions like partners and sales channels.

Sales and sales development

An MI report that provides you with sales data is essential when you deploy new rates. When you go live, you need to see how sales are developing. Too often this is hampered by issues with sales development due to customers having several days between obtaining a quote or renewal invite and deciding whether to buy the policy. To overcome this, you need to have sales development charts that show sales as they develop with comparisons between A/B test groups and earlier time periods. This makes it much easier to understand the impact of new rates at early durations. It's the same with your renewals. You send out your renewal price ahead of the date the policy is due to renew. You should have renewal development that properly shows sales development and lapse development. This reduces your information uncertainty due to sales and renewal delays.

Tactical changes

Conversion reports are a powerful tool post-deployment for tweaking rates and controlling exposure. All of what you do comes with uncertainty, so if conversion is running high for a segment then it may be that anti-selection is at work. An adjustment to the rates to increase prices for that segment can ensure there are no issues. Similarly, where conversion is low it may be that opportunities are being missed and a reduction in rates is appropriate.

Market prices

This is a powerful tool in markets and jurisdictions where market prices are available. Comparing your own rates to what you forecast as the market premium or what you see as the actual market premium will tell you a lot about your position. It gives you a measure of your competitiveness and an idea about the extent to which your brand carries your rate. You can also see if you are keeping pace with market rate inflation.

Benchmarking

Both market data and external data can be used to understand how your exposure compares to what is available in the market. In the UK for example, DVLA data can be used to see which vehicles are on the roads. This can then be compared to your own exposure to understand where you are under- or overexposed. It allows you to assess whether you are achieving the right mix of business and identify which opportunities you are missing out on (intentionally or not) due to underwriting footprint rules. Census data can be used to assess the overall available distribution in the market of ages of drivers. Again, comparing this to your own exposure and considering what you want to write tells you if you are over- or underexposed, and much like with conversion reports, you can use this to adjust your prices, helping you to deal with the inherent uncertainty of setting prices. The same is true for other lines of business. Data on holiday destinations can be used to understand one's footprint in travel insurance.

Automation

Methods have been emerging for automated monitoring. This is especially useful for segmented analysis, such as conversion reports, where there is a lot of information and it would be difficult to sift through all of it regularly. Systems can be instructed to flag when conversions in segments over a given volume fall below or rise above the specific threshold, allowing you to benefit from the advantages of this analysis without making the difficult and laborious time commitment that is required.

The importance of setting up your data correctly

If you've set up your data as I explained in Chapter Four, you'll have nice pricing ledgers and your MI will be a breeze. The MI simply generates reports that are based on that data, which is why it's so important to put the work in early on to get the data where you want it to be. If you're regularly having to ask people to do any form of coding or processing to find out information for you, then either your data's not set up correctly or you're not receiving the MI you need. The same goes for your team: if they're regularly having to go back to the data to rebuild things or re-report on them, then again, you haven't set up your MI properly.

The great advantage in pricing reporting is that production is an automatable, repeatable process, so creating the reports in a way that means it can be done again and again is incredibly efficient. As is so often the case with IT and MI, it's easier to do this for everything than to do it ad hoc, which ideally you want to avoid. If people do have to do ad hoc processing because the data isn't available to them, then that should be fed back to the person responsible to ensure that the information is made available to them in the future. You should encourage the build for an ad hoc process to be done and then productionised, thereby making it part of processes in future.

What makes an MI report useful?

Pricing MI reports is especially useful for sales. The whole business is based on sales and these need to be tracked correctly. You'll want to know your conversion rates, your renewal rates and your retention information, and you'll need to understand loss ratios as they come through. It's important to see how much you're paying out in claims, both capped and uncapped figures. It's useful to look at capped figures and also to look at a range of caps, and it's important not to forget about the large claims. Seeing how things are developing and basing forecasts on these development charts will help you make confident predictions.

Being able to automatically develop forecasts and complete your other reporting responsibilities is key to the ultimate goals of any insurer. Having good, clean, fresh data and accurate MI reporting is instrumental in achieving this.

Once you have your MI data together, you'll be able to review it regularly and ensure that the information flows to the right people. Ideally, it should be someone's responsibility to review it, and you could set up some form of automatic monitoring so that the system will flag if things are not working how you want them to. This should involve emergency flagging too. For example, if your total conversion suddenly drops, you'll need to have that flagged as soon as it happens. If you're not aware of it, then the loss in sales over even a day could significantly hurt an annual plan. Similarly, when you're dealing with the loss ratios, it's good to have a notification of large losses when they come in, and the same goes for your renewal volumes.

You should also set up some committees to review the information: a weekly sales committee and a monthly technical committee that reviews the MI and understands whether the business is following your plan are recommended. You also want to make sure there's information flowing upwards so that senior people are seeing useful information. This is likely to require working with your finance and other teams to agree on the sources and formats of data to ensure it is accurate and useful.

Results sometimes deteriorate. The world changes, markets move, competitors change. You need to know this quickly and you need an answer as to why things have changed. Ideally, it should always be pricing that notices this first. Pricing is often the most immediate lever that can be moved to control performance. When results do deteriorate, people will be looking to you for a plan to solve the problem, and someone from pricing will need to investigate. It could be that your sales have dropped substantially, or that your claims frequency has risen suddenly, or perhaps your past claims have deteriorated. Having MI already available can make a massive difference to how quickly you can do that. Quick and decisive action will mark you out as a competent leader. Confused reports and delays in putting data and reports together will not.

It's important to note that once you've got this set up, you might not be looking at it every day, but when you do need to, having it there can improve your operations.

Forecasting

Once you've got the information you need, you can then use it for forecasting, which is an important function of the pricing team, be it for impact analysis or financial plans. The pricing team is often asked to feed into the business planning of the organisation. Typically, an organisation will have a three- to five-year plan, with differing levels of detail. It's nearly always the pricing team's responsibility to monitor how their work is delivering against that plan and to then feed back to the finance team to let them know whether things are going to plan or not.

The MI is important in achieving that forecasting and re-forecasting, so you need to be able to fold numbers from the plan into your MI and vice versa so that you can monitor those in a sensible way that is easy to digest. Otherwise, your team ends up having to spend time trying to look at the numbers from finance that might be in a different format and then comparing them to the MI. Coming up with an automated way of getting the finance data in that forecast can make a big difference to your ability to achieve those numbers for the business, which is a complicated process.

Getting this right and always knowing what's going on in the business is important. Getting to grips with how effective your prices are and how that works for each individual customer, not just averages, is vital. When you set this up properly, you'll see the impact of your pricing on particular types of customers. You can then decide whether you need to move your prices.

A word of warning on forecasting. Models are mathematical representations of the behaviour of humans. Reducing human behaviour to fairly simple equations is an act of throwing away a lot of information in order to create a simple formula for forecasting. This is necessary to make progress and is useful but it only captures an essence of the things that led to a claim or the customer to buy or not to buy their policy. When we use them for forecasting, we are implicitly assuming that people will behave in the way that they do in the models. In economics this has become known as assuming the existence of the economic person aka homo economicus. That is people who behave how they do in the models. The real world is far more complicated, and humans are driven by far more than is captured in models. We should always be aware that models are for homo insuralis and not real people.

MI can also be used to monitor the effectiveness of your risk premiums. The Gini index is a way of monitoring whether your models work well and there are quite a lot of different diagnostics for measuring whether your prices are effective compared to the information that's coming through, which is ultimately what you want to know. Are your prices working all of the time for everyone they're meant to be working for? Are you charging every customer the exact right price to achieve your goals?

Being able to demonstrate that you're regularly considering how your prices affect your customers and whether those customers are being charged a fair and reasonable premium for their insurance is going to become more and more important, and you need MI to understand that.

Sometimes the prices you set will not deliver as well as you were hoping and you need to be honest about that by showing it in the commentary and saying that things have not worked as well as you wanted them to, or indeed showing where things have been effective. If you've delivered well, making that clear in the commentary gives you an opportunity to shine. You should also use this to showcase the value of your team to senior people within the organisation.

CASE STUDY: The problem with having incorrect data

In a hypothetical example an insurer might want to develop an MI pack for their executive due to the frustrations of executives being unable to get useful MI. Simple things like how much premium had been sold recently on a particular account might not be available easily. When needed, people would have to go away, process the data and put it together as an ad hoc report. Sometimes this would conflict with other reports, which is obviously time-consuming and a waste of resources. It would also cause confusion and suboptimal decisions.

The executive would want a computerised MI system at their fingertips so they could access all the information for running the organisation. To do this, they would need to put a project in place.

It could turn out, for a fairly substantial amount of the business, the information the executive wants isn't available. It might not be collected or might not be provided by partners (or a selection of other reasons).

Now the problem would be exacerbated if instead of throwing up their hands and tackling the root of the problems, the hypothetical leadership team tasked the project leaders with making sense of the data they had instead. The project leaders would have to think of clever ways they could make what they had look like what they wanted.

The MI may become fictional because it isn't using the real numbers. The data might look nice when presented in charts, but it isn't true and as soon as people started asking questions about it, it just confuses things even more. A lot of effort would go into making the figures *seem* right rather than *be* right.

What actually needs to be done is the real hard work of getting accurate data.

This demonstrates why it's so important to build solid foundations for your data before trying to do anything else. Typically, the bigger the organisation, the more people there are who aren't attached to the detail and the easier it is to end up in a world where you've got something that's not real or true.

CASE STUDY: Getting the MI right

Providers who are aiming to move to a new system and clean up their data should spend time aligning their figures with the figures from finance until they get to a point where they comfortably match. This is before building the MI parts. They build up the data insights so that they can look at the figures, daily, weekly, monthly and annually and then for all the add-ons, and then cross-reference these so they can see where they had been allocated by both teams. This means that they can look at the data from both a pricing and a financial standpoint, and they are then able to build out all the reports and know they are populated with accurate and trustworthy data.

Having done that, they can use the new source for the reporting that goes into the committees for understanding customer outcomes, and understanding the sales of the business and how claims are developing, with the result that they can view the figures across multiple bases and thus pick up on any problems ahead.

The data should also be automated so it is possible to see, with just a few clicks, the details of any sales that had been made previously, and everything is always up to date. From this, an executive pack can be set up to be automatically produced in time for committee meetings and thus reduce the burden on people who would usually have to process these.

This might all seem mundane, but it's imperative that you do this if you want to have a real handle on your data. Getting to a position where you can go into your system and pull out the sales data and break that down by the different ratings factors is what will ultimately improve your business operations, and although it might seem like hard work to get there, once it's done everything will be much easier.

Sooner or later you'll find that you're not hitting your targets and then you'll suddenly need to find the relevant information in a hurry, and this is going to be stressful and difficult if you don't have the correct information to hand.

EXERCISE: Your sales data

1. Can you find out what your sales were for yesterday?
2. If you can, will the figures match exactly with the figures from the finance team?
3. If they don't match, do you know why?

If you can't answer these three questions, then you need to do some work.

Summary

You can see why organising your data early on is so important for your later analysis. Setting up regular MI reports that contain the information that is needed to monitor and control the sales and loss ratio provides the levers to effectively run the book. Getting this information flowing automatically at regular intervals is a substantial advantage. Analysis is sometimes overshadowed by other steps but it is a powerful tool especially when uncertainty is running high. Tactical changes can be made very quickly to control the performance and react to changing conditions much faster than can be achieved with the less flexible methods.

Utilising information about market prices and benchmarks can be another tool in controlling the performance and making good choices on how to set prices. Some items can be automated to prevent you drowning in charts while also still being able to react using analysis.

Analysis shows why we need to set up our data as described, and having our data already set up means analysis can flow in near-real time and you can be confident it is correct. If it's not correctly populated, then it's not going to benefit your business and could in fact harm it.

Quality data and good analytical skills and functions allow you to get your forecasting right. Quality forecasting reduces uncertainty and puts us in the driving seat of the performance. A lack of analysis can force us to be reactive to performance and events. Often this means that we do not have time to take the necessary action, which would result in missing our sales and profit targets.

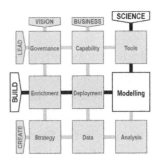

8
Modelling

In this chapter I'll explore modelling and explain why it gets so much attention. While it is important, we should also accept that the best model of the past is only as good as what it says about the future and what we can use it for. When it comes to modelling, we should ask ourselves 'Does it make the boat go faster?', by which we mean 'Is it getting us any closer to our achieving our objectives?'[5] If the answer is no then we should explore other routes of improvement that will.

I have long believed, and I think many would agree with me, that having more external data is more effective than having more complicated models.

5   'The GB Men's Eight', Will It Make The Boat Go Faster? (no date),
     https://willitmaketheboatgofaster.com/about, accessed
     12 December 2023

Modelling is perhaps not as important as the other subjects I talk about in this book, yet in existing published literature modelling is by a large margin the most discussed topic, almost the *only* topic. If I ordered the steps in the Price Writer method by the amount of existing material there is about each one, modelling would be at the top with a large gap between that and the next item on the list.

Start by asking yourself a difficult rhetorical question: 'Have I seen a worthwhile improvement in sales, profitability or customer outcomes from rebuilding an existing model with a different algorithm?' That is, 'Have I seen a genuine significant improvement in the end results for something I already have that gets me closer to the objective – improvements that make the boat go faster, not just apparent improvements in statistical measures?' If you have then that's great, but also ask yourself if the benefit was worthwhile compared to the work and any difficulties involved.

You should view modelling as being about using the right tool for each job. It is not a staircase you need to climb with some models at the bottom and some at the top. You don't need a plan to use the most complicated algorithms as long as you are using appropriate statistical analysis for what you are doing. There are often only minor benefits to changing algorithms, which is not to say you shouldn't do so when it is worthwhile or when a different tool is more appropriate, but you should work out your priorities based on expected benefits. You need to get closer to the goal, not dive into greater complexity as if that is an end goal in its own right. Minor statistical improvements may be lost to many other complications in the pricing process; for example, enrichment and deployment improvements often bring more benefit so we should consider whether to prioritise those.

I often feel that there is a shiny object mentality when it comes to modelling. Some people are continually distracted by a rush towards more complexity, as if complexity itself is the strategy or the objective. They are often so firmly and unyieldingly convinced this is the case that the distraction comes at the expense of what's already planned or underway. A good strategy can avoid this problem, as can recognising what is happening and setting firm requirements to achieve concrete objectives.

Explainability and the two types of modelling

While there are many ways to categorise models, your key considerations should be the level to which you understand how the price relates to the cost of manufacturing and providing the product, and whether you can explain to a customer, stakeholder, regulator or other interested party how the price has been arrived at and how this matches the cost to manufacture. This is often called explainability. With the cost to manufacture, you are not only considering the cost of claims and expenses on a narrow definition or single-year basis – it can be much more complicated than that.

You can consider all of the costs and the whole lifetime, which also means that, to name a few, administration, acquisition and cancellation costs can be amortised or given other appropriate treatments, as can commissions. There is no reason why you can't vary the prices in layers similar to market pricing, or optimise them for lifetime value and within sensible constraints and objectives. You do also need to recognise that you must be able to explain the link between the price and the cost to manufacture the customer's product. As long as you can adequately do that, you can set the prices using any of these techniques and others. Prices do not have to be linked only to the narrow one-year expenses and expected claim costs.

The biggest mistake I see people make with explainability is not realising it means explainability to a customer, stakeholder, regulator, board member or other interested party rather than to another statistician. You know how the modelling works, so explainability to someone who also knows how it works is interesting but not the point. You need to understand the rates yourself but you can largely do that by understanding the mathematics. You don't need to explain every price and every transition before prices go live, but you should have processes in place that lead you to methods and prices you could explain to outsiders if necessary. Explain does not mean trotting out statistics – that is useless to a non-statistician and they are the people to whom you need to explain how the price is arrived at, what evidence and knowledge you have that it is the right price, and why prices move in the way that they do in the particular circumstances if those involve a transition between prices or even a transition in customer details that is not expected.

Too often explainability is turned into an exercise in statistics when it is an exercise in proof and narrative. For people who are not statisticians, using more complicated or deeper statistics to 'explain' the prices is unhelpful. There are two types of effective explanation:

1. Evidence-based explanation that demonstrates a clear link between what you observe to be the cost to you of manufacturing the product and the price charged.

2. Narrative explanation that links the characteristics of what is being insured to the different levels of the prices. This is not the same as using simple intuition. Simple intuition is sometimes misleading, but it is about our ability to understand a process related to the items insured that explains how the prices change for different characteristics.

This leads to the two ways to categorise models:

1. **Group one modelling** – The transitions are explainable. You can demonstrate the link between the price and the cost to manufacture and supply the product (in particular when customers change their details), which can also be seen as the movement between states that will move their price, such as changing property, vehicle, staff numbers or other attributes. With group one modelling, you understand why the change has happened, and you can either explain it or provide evidence that can be understood by a non-statistician. Another example might be when a customer renews their policy. You usually have to age their details so they get a year older, and they hopefully obtain an extra year's no-claims discount (bonus-malus), unless of course they've had a claim. Their business gets older, their property gets older and so on. At the point of renewal you can easily pick apart those different items that have led to the price change.

2. **Group two modelling** – This is where you can't explain the price movement; for example, when the customer changes property or vehicles, or the policy ages, you don't understand the price movement and you can't show evidence of the link between the price change and the delta in the cost to manufacture the product. You can't say how much is caused by underlying factors

like the type of business, socio-demographics or other attributes; you only know that the price has changed. You can't explain why to yourself, stakeholders or the customer. You can't apply any outside knowledge to check if you are comfortable with the change.

Good explanations are narrative- or evidence-based; bad explanations rely on complicated statistics or fall back on vague phrases like 'We use sophisticated algorithms.'

To be absolutely clear, it is pretty much impossible to do a desktop exercise and put all of the different algorithms and different ways of modelling into either group one or group two based only on the mathematics and nothing else. Different methods and algorithms will be in different groups depending on the circumstances, which include but are not limited to:

- The product under investigation

- Data considerations like the amount of data and the time period it covers

- Situational considerations like the exposure and response – for example, the peril in risk modelling or the process in demand modelling

- Resource considerations like how much time and resources you have for the investigation and what knowledge you have of the product and peril

Problems that arise here are often not because of the modelling algorithm, though it is common to blame it. Most commonly, the problems are driven by your understanding of the data and your knowledge of the process, product and peril. More knowledge and analysis lead to more explainability and better prices.

Scoring models

You should score models in the circumstances on their ability to achieve the objective and their alignment with the strategy. For example, if you used the criteria you set up in the chapter on strategy, you would ask the question 'What is the purpose of a pricing team?' and arrive at the answer 'To find the right price, to hit financial targets and to avoid anti-selection and moral hazard.' You want to make sure you're competitive, sustainable, compliant with regulations and that you deliver the customer price outcomes.

Do models from group one or group two particularly help you find the right price? Both groups contain models that are effective in this regard. The only reason to prefer any model over another is in terms of its performance, and most likely you could find models in group one that perform as well as group two. That said, you should remember that performance means sales, profitability, and company and customer outcomes, not just statistics, so there is little point in considering group two models unless they really will perform sufficiently better to warrant the other difficulties. You can usually find the right price while retaining explainability.

It's a similar story when it comes to hitting financial targets. You can achieve those with models you understand and can communicate to customers, stakeholders, regulators and others.

It's also the same when avoiding anti-selection and moral hazard, and when being competitive, sustainable and compliant with regulations. There is no particular way of mathematically calculating a price that is or isn't compliant with regulations, unless the regulations stipulate this. A mathematical formula cannot itself be problematic in that way, so you've not got a reason to prefer one group of models over the other on that basis, although it's typical in regulations to need to be able to demonstrate either how you set prices or that you understand the prices you are setting, and also to be able to communicate how you arrive at your prices, so group one dominates here as well.

Generally, you would prefer to use group one modelling under the regulatory environments that are common for insurance throughout the world where you have to send your rates into the regulator for them to review. In this scenario, you can only really use group one models because you have to be able to show someone how every price is derived. Models from group two, which are opaque and difficult to understand in that regard, just aren't appropriate for environments like that. As another example, for principle-based regulatory systems, group one is preferable for much the same reasons.

Delivering price outcomes

You also need to deliver the customer price outcomes that align to your company's policy. Should a customer feel unhappy with their price and contact customer services for some form of explanation, it can be difficult to provide that with group one models, but it is near impossible with group two.

Although you have made rates that you understand well, they can sometimes move in ways that make sense statistically but which might not make sense to the customer. A common example of this is burglar alarms in property insurance. Unfortunately, having a burglar alarm usually means that if somebody is burgled, the cost of that burglary is more than for somebody who does not have an alarm, probably because they have more valuable possessions. This is not always offset by lower frequency, meaning their insurance will cost more than it would for someone without a burglar alarm, which is not what a customer expects. They would not expect to tell you that they've had a burglar alarm fitted and for you to then tell them that their insurance price has gone up as a result. GI is riddled with situations like this.

The statistics strongly tell a story that conflicts with customer expectations and your own intuition, and this complexity is a key reason why you need to use statistical modelling. With group one models, you have the ability to understand and explain the process, either through narrative or through clear and understandable evidence.

Under group two models you won't have any information about what drives the price change, only that it has happened. You only know to charge a different price because your model tells you to. It tells you what to price but you can't explain it to a customer because you don't have that information. Life is not a static thing. The world is continuously changing, so being able to look at your model and understand it is important. You need to be able to adjust models with outside knowledge and allow for a changing world or underlying circumstances. With group one models, you can make those changes, and you can use your and others' knowledge and experience to adjust them, which is difficult with group two models.

If a group two model is going to perform genuinely better than any available group one model, then that is a perfectly sensible time to use it. By perform better I mean improve sales, profitability, or company and customer outcomes so much that it outweighs the downsides, not just in explainability but also in deployment and other complexities.

This is likely to be only when the model forms part of back-end processes and not when it directly determines end customer prices; for example, if you wanted to categorise a large amount of external data. It's fairly common to have a lot of data points about the geography of what you're insuring. If you want to condense this information to simplify it or you want some level of smoothing over geographic areas, you'll want to turn that into a single, continuous factor and order a particular rated group from your lowest risk to your highest risk. There would be no issue with using a group two model if that is most appropriate, although group one is still preferred. The same considerations apply when investigating residuals: a group two model needs to be genuinely better than any group one model that could do the same job. If the lack of explainability of the group two model is not offset by better results, then it should not be used.

With group two you don't understand how all the variables relate to each other, so this type of modelling is sometimes acceptable for vehicle-related areas too. There are some things you might want to directly rate that clearly affect the risk, such as the top speed of the vehicle; however, there are lots of smaller, less powerful factors that might be quite complicated to analyse, in which case you can use dimensionality reduction models and clustering.

There is some debate as to the value of smoothing your rates by geographic areas. Not many people move house to an adjacent postcode or an adjacent house, so it doesn't matter if the price changes by a lot between these areas, although it does seem sensible to use information from nearby areas to inform rating. You add in your adjacency or longitude and latitude information with appropriate break points so that you end up with smoothly changing prices between different areas, which can be important for the customer experience and reducing uncertainty.

The live environment

It is important to do everything you can to get your modelling environment to align with your live environment. This can be difficult but you will pay dearly for problems here – it is probably the source of most deployment errors and issues. If that's a concern and you feel that putting 200 new variables into your live environment is too big a step, then crunching those down into one nice smooth rating factor can make a big difference too.

Ultimately you may not need to understand how different vehicles, for example, relate to each other. If you've got a huge sample space of all the many attributes you could have about cars, like their weight, their power, their height, their size, their seats and so on, you don't need to explain all of the differences between them, but you do need to understand how your customer prices relate to the cost of manufacturing the product. Good understanding of those drivers is needed, not tedious detail, so using a form of dimensionality reduction in that situation, even if you have assessed it as a group two model, is fine if it is the most appropriate.

Should you find a group two model is the best on the given criteria, then be aware that even setting your prices and checking they are correct will be more challenging. A lack of transparency would be a good reason for concern both inside and outside of a pricing team about the way we set prices, which should always come down to data and knowledge, not the model. Your ability to explain pricing to someone is difficult to do with a group one model, but almost impossible with a group two model.

There are other factors to consider with pricing and there are still concerns over how you use the data you have. Customer age, for example, could be problematic despite its ubiquitous use. There are plenty of rules about age discrimination in many countries, but in most of them it remains legal to use age to alter somebody's prices. Should a customer's price increase when they get older, they might question why. In this situation, it's good to be able to explain and show statistically that older people have more car crashes, or more theft claims, or more escapes of water or more fires. A group two model would make that explanation and understanding difficult; you couldn't know what is happening and you might not be confident that as a company you are compliant with laws and regulations.

Reviews and refreshes

There is a simple answer to how often to review and refresh models. It should happen:

- When there is a need to make a change; for example, a system migration
- When there is a meaningful change, like new features or external data to add
- On a regular basis, such as annually

It is possible to set up complicated monitoring to assess whether models are still effective. This can be interesting MI but rarely fits well with model refresh planning because it is difficult to refresh models out of synch. The resources versus outcome payoff that this produces is also debatable, so a regular update on a well-understood schedule is more effective and sensible from a planning standpoint.

EXERCISE: Learning from complaints

1. Analyse your pricing complaints to help you improve your customer outcomes and your customer experience.

2. What in particular are your customers concerned about?

3. Review the information that's being shared with customers when they query prices.

4. Are you comfortable with the information that's being provided?

5. Remember, anything that's told to a customer is then public and could end up anywhere. Even if it comes from a customer service agent, should a customer later query it or refer it to the ombudsman or the regulator, pricing are likely to be asked questions about it. Are you comfortable with what the customer is being told? Can you provide some better guidance for your customer service agents when it comes to price?

Summary

Modelling is about choosing the right tool for the job, and it should not be confused with the objective. The only thing that really matters is the real-world sales and profitability of what you deploy. Modelling for modelling's sake and theoretical improvements in statical measures mean nothing if they are not translated into real meaningful and measurable impacts against the objectives, which often means beneficial effects on profit or sales.

Explainability of our prices means being able to explain to a non-statistician how they are arrived at.

Usually by linking them to the cost to serve the customer, either through a narrative or using proof. You need to make sure you use techniques that lead you to prices that you could explain to a customer, regulator, stakeholder, board member or other interested party if you are required to do so.

Before modelling you need to assess your available modelling techniques to ascertain which ones will create prices you would be able to explain, and which ones could create prices that you will struggle to explain. This is not a desktop exercise because explainability is a moving target depending on your own circumstances.

You can see that although modelling should not be prioritised in the way it usually is, it's still a vital part of your role as a pricing team, and your choice of modelling will have a huge impact on your ability to explain things to your stakeholders. Try not to be drawn into shiny object syndrome; instead stay focused on the objectives, strategy, and tactics.

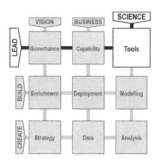

	VISION	BUSINESS	SCIENCE
LEAD	Governance	Capability	**Tools**
BUILD	Enrichment	Deployment	Modelling
CREATE	Strategy	Data	Analysis

9

Tools

In this chapter we'll explore the systems, processes and tools that are available, and consider which are best for your organisation. I'll ask you to consider which is most appropriate for the needs of your organisation, both now and in the future.

The most common systems you need to work with are a PAS, a claim system and a quotes system (if this is separate from the policy system). The most common item of software you'll need as a pricing team is your rating engine. You may also have other systems for analysis and modelling. There are quite a few different types of rating engine available and some companies have their own bespoke versions, but at its core a rating engine is a piece of software that, when sent a request, returns a result with the prices.

Generally, with rating engine tools, you have the choice of using a bespoke or an off-the-shelf system, or continuing with whatever system you currently have. Even if you decide not to change, you are making an implicit choice, which is important to recognise. You should be asking yourself whether the system you're currently using is the best one for your purposes or you're sticking with it just because it's what you've already got.

For a long time there were just two off-the-shelf systems available. Over recent years, there's been quite an explosion in the market and more are being introduced every year. There are now a lot of options and each one will cater to different types of insurer and be targeted towards different people and different types of organisation, so you can get a pretty decent off-the-shelf system that's tailored to your needs.

When you consider the systems and software you use, it's important to ask questions like 'What controls does the team have over that system?', 'Who can set and change the prices?' and 'Who's authorised to implement changes?'

Bespoke or off the shelf?

If you work in areas where you produce mostly online rates, and particularly if you work a lot through websites, you might well need to be returning your prices in fractions of a second to meet the service-level agreements you'll have with those platforms and providers. Off-the-shelf systems will be fine for dealing with that, but you'll have to make a judgement call as to what type of system is right for you.

Some systems are best targeted at speciality insurance or bespoke insurers and areas where products aren't particularly standardised; others are built for a mass market and are tailored to produce large complicated prices and process them quickly.

Off-the-shelf systems are often easier to work with when it comes to controls because they have a lot of options built in. For example, you can set your users and decide whether someone should have to sign off. Bespoke systems typically have these options too, but they're less flexible and it's up to the organisation to decide the permissions and content. Many off-the-shelf systems come with excellent record-keeping, so you can see who's made changes to each part of the rates and when they did it. Because the system often stores all the previous versions of the data, you can go through and see how pricing elements have changed over time, who made the changes and when they were made.

There are also some good-quality audit tools that will help pricing teams understand changes and these make it easy to record information. Some tools will even communicate automatically with the team when the rates are set to update. They can send a message to affected parties when your rates go live, send warnings in advance of a rates change, and you can also record quality logs with them. In addition, you can set permissions so that people outside of the pricing team have access to the information. This makes communications between teams much easier.

One of the issues that often come up is that the systems you use are determined by two things: what the people in your team know how to use and what you're already using. This puts startups in particular at a huge disadvantage because they are new and don't have systems in place. What startups often have as a genuine advantage is that they're not buried under legacy ways of doing things, which means they can be flexible in the choices they make.

On-rail and open systems

There are two types of system that you can implement in your team: open and on-rail.

An open system enables you to build anything you like and you usually start with an empty space. There's a big overhead when you start with this type of system because you have to build it from scratch, whereas on-rail systems lack some flexibility (which you may be able to overcome) but have the structure already set up for you. Some on-rail systems can also create your

MI for you, which historically rating engines haven't been the best at. You can directly connect them to your existing systems and some will happily work with your bespoke paths or your bespoke claims systems.

Both types may need to be integrated with your internal systems, otherwise you will need to move around large files in pricing, which is often quite awkward to do. Integrating directly with your data systems can make a big difference in efficiency and security for you as a pricing team.

With on-rail systems you'll work through a set of things that you want to include in your prices – for example, your risk layer. You build this layer, you add your expenses and your market layer, and then you build up each layer. You can turn on and turn off different elements until you get it working in the way you need it to for your team.

Open systems are flexible systems that are completely open, which means you have to build everything yourself. There are components there, and there are sometimes tutorials and examples, but building one can entail a lot of work. If you've been using them for a few years, you might well have built large rates and it can become quite difficult to document those in a meaningful way and move on. It's hard to migrate between any of these systems because you can't just pick up your rates and drop them into a different system, they don't talk to each other in that way.

Support is also an important consideration. Some providers give pretty much instant chat support and this is built into the software. With others you'll have to send emails, and with some of the older legacy providers it's still the case that you'll send an email and will have to wait quite a few days to receive a reply.

Cloud or on-premises?

This leads to questions about whether to have cloud-based or on-premises software. The trend is moving towards the cloud, and with things like rating engines it makes sense to have them in the cloud. You might well find that other systems like the PAS are already in cloud spaces and, certainly when you're dealing with requests coming in from websites, those will often be cloud-based.

With rating engines, it's almost always the case that cloud-based systems are better. Processing huge amounts of complicated data can be exceedingly cumbersome on local machines. Virtual machines on-premises or in the cloud can overcome many issues, though even these can struggle. For data systems, the cloud may be better, but not necessarily. This probably seems like a contrarian view because there's a lot of pressure to move everything towards the cloud, but you need to take the time to work out what's right for you and get the expert advice you need – don't be pushed into following the crowd. The cloud is typically good for things like scalability, so adding more resourcing, more processing power, more memory, more storage etc is easily done but it's worth remembering that you're often processing huge amounts of data. On the one hand, it's good to have a lot of IT power available for that, but on the other hand, you're paying every time you process something. This means that you could find that in pricing you're generating massive bills compared to the rest of the organisation because you're continually processing models. No one wants to find themself in a position where they have to think twice about fitting a model or investigating something because of the cost of the IT resources.

Another consideration is how much legacy data you've got and how you deal with that. For the rest of the organisation, anything that's past data, like closed claims, old policies etc, is not often needed day to day. They might only need a summary of it, or they might not need it at all. For those departments, the data can go into cold storage to meet your regulatory requirements. You might need to access it at a later date – for example, when dealing with complaints. Pricing, however, relies on a lot of this past data, and in some cases you could have to go back through years and years' worth of massive tables. This means you could find yourself in a situation whereby you've got new data in the cloud and a huge amount of data on-premises and you'll need to use both.

Legacy systems

Often the reason you stay on a legacy system is because you're stuck with it, and you're stuck with it for a few reasons. Your team know how to use it, so they're going to be reluctant to change, and you've already built lots of your own resources and infrastructure into those pieces of software. You can end up in a legacy situation with the cloud – the two are not mutually exclusive. It is extremely hard to move between cloud providers, and it's not in the interest of cloud providers or rating engine providers to make this any easier for you.

Once you're with Google, it's difficult to then move to Amazon or Microsoft. It's also worth remembering that while these providers appear cheap at the moment, the business model of a lot of these mega corporations has been what we'd term 'lock and load'. They get people stuck in and then load up their prices, which is something you need to be aware of as it could well happen to you in the future.

People often talk about how it's easier to add new software in the cloud, but it's also quite easy to do that on-premises nowadays. IT teams often have good application management tools and there are options to integrate hybrid models.

162

Merging systems

Something I've seen done quite well is converting new data systems so that you can flip them into the old format and flip your old data into the new formats. This means you can use both in either place, although you still have to migrate what is often quite large on-premises data into the cloud so that you can join the two together and do the analytical work. Some insurers will find that easy, but others might well find it difficult. You might find that you're having conversations with other parts of the business about the need to have all the legacy data and be challenged on it, because your needs will be different to the needs of other areas.

You can see that it's not clear-cut and there are quite a few considerations about whether on-premises or cloud is better. This will depend on the size of your book, the amount of past data you've got, the number of lines of business you've got and the complexity of your products, among other things.

Often people talk about the cloud as if it's something everyone should be using and always means the same thing. In reality, cloud means quite a few different things. It could refer to virtual machines or to an entire estate, or it could refer to applications provided by third parties.

If your organisation has a fairly efficient IT department, then it might be that over the long term on-premises is a good option for you. Having a good IT department might be better, in some cases, than using the cloud. For large insurers in particular, the advantages of the cloud infrastructure might not materialise as much as you expect; however, for a small insurer, where buying significant amounts of infrastructure would mean a significant cost upfront, it makes much more sense to use the cloud.

Software

In the past few years many great pieces of software have been launched that will help in-house teams collaborate better, and they can make it much easier to work together with teams across the organisation. These online tools are particularly suited to a world where we want either hybrid or fully remote working practices. The great thing about these modern tools is that they're easily shared, so a lot of people can see what they're doing in real time.

Task management and project management software

There are some clever task management and project management tools for organising things like meetings, team calendars and repeat processes, which enable your team to keep up to date with what they're meant to be doing and you to keep up to date with where they are without needing to have meetings. You can also keep minutes and organise your team more efficiently.

EXERCISE: Your choice of software

Fill in these three sentences:

1. We chose our IT infrastructure because...
2. We chose our data set-up because...
3. We chose our pricing software because...

Scripting and open-source software

In the insurance industry, particularly if you're working with data, it's common to find people both inside and outside of pricing with skills in SQL, for example. With modelling, it's usual to have people with skills in Python. Even so, it's much harder to audit and check coded work than it is to audit and check point-and-click work.

Auditing scripted solutions is difficult and making sure they're properly tested can be challenging. To most, it's challenging enough when using off-the-shelf options; it's even harder when choosing the open-source solutions. For this reason, you need to carry out a proper analysis before diving into using any tool. It isn't enough just to consider the current skills you have within your team, you also need to look at the skills available in the rest of the organisation. For example, what skills are available for testing and checking the implementation and integration with other systems? I often find that people argue over which is the best open-source software to use and entirely forget to consider whether the software is in fact the right tool to use in the first place. It is rather like arguing over which colour of spanner to use.

SQL is commonly used but it has a lot of variance, and it seems like there's more being added all the time. Roughly speaking, it works in the same way for everyone but there are nuances which make it a better fit for some organisations than others. If you take on new people in your data engineering team, they will happily take on SQL but you should avoid picking languages in environments where only a small number, maybe only one person, knows how to use it. You should also avoid choosing a solution simply because it's someone's favourite. You might well be stuck for a long time with whatever you choose at this point, and potentially people will be stuck with it long after you've moved on from your organisation. You should therefore think carefully about what the best options are for your specific circumstances both now and in the long term.

Modelling solutions

There are also software solutions that are solely for modelling. If you work in a pricing department where you hand everything over to an IT team for deployment, then you could choose a solution like this.

I would, however, caution against this approach because over the course of the past fifteen to twenty years the pricing team has gone from being a scientific department that analyses things and then hands that information over to operational teams to being an operational team which is at the heart of an organisation. While not every insurer is there, the direction of travel is certainly towards every pricing department being an operational department themself – in effect a department that's made up of operations, IT and analytical people.

If you choose a system that can only do the analysis for you and you then have to hand it over to IT, eventually that IT work is going to land in pricing anyway, and at that point you will probably wish you'd invested in a rating engine from the start, although even then it's prone to deployment problems. Ultimately it doesn't matter how good your model is if there are errors in how it's deployed. Poor deployment will ruin all of the power you've worked so hard to build.

Unfortunately, however you transpose the work coming out of one system and into another there are

167

risks, and even if it's done in a highly automated way through some form of integration, there are still risks present. You also need to bear in mind that if you do want to integrate systems, your IT team will have to build some way to do this. This means you'll have a nice fancy system to do your analysis in but then at some point you'll have to download the results. Sometimes this could be through XML or JSON but it could easily be to Excel, which is hardly high-tech and also prone to errors.

My advice is to go straight to a rating engine but to always assess your particular circumstances and decide what's best for your team. I suspect if you're looking towards the future and thinking about what your needs might be further down the road, you are likely to find that the best solution is a rating engine that can do your analytics and potentially also your MI.

Different IT systems

You have a choice of which IT system to use, including the following:

- **Open point and click** – You have an environment where you set everything up by building pricing components from a library of what is available and those components are wired together into a process. It is usually possible to code variables using a library of formulas. The environment may include price setting tools or these could be imported from another application. While this allows for a lot of flexibility in how prices are set, it also requires a lot of work to set up. Over time, rates can become complicated and it can be difficult to get an overall sense of how all the components operate together.

- **On-rail point and click** – In these applications you lose some flexibility, but you don't have to do as much development. Often there is a section of the application for the main tasks like MI, risk premium, optimisation, expenses, and the other layers of the prices and process. You connect your data into the system and it is already set up to provide these things, which you build as you want to without any need to wire them together. It is possible to use many methods to set prices but there could be less flexibility on how different algorithms interact and work together. MI is readily available but may not be entirely customisable. Optimisation and lifetime value may require only a few clicks to implement, but it may not be possible to make adjustments to how these operate, which could prevent you from adding more complexity or bespoke elements. That said, for many people what is lost in flexibility is made up for in lower resource needs.

- **Even more flexible systems** – You enter in the data and do all the calculations yourself. This means you're free to build things how you want to. This approach is better for people with big teams and potentially when you have people who are skilled in using those particular tools. While it may still be point and click, in some places there are also complicated formulas that can be set, with many areas interacting and crossing over in the process.

- **Scripted** – There are some totally scripted options and this can work well for some firms. The prices are written entirely as computer code, possibly with reference to tables and existing files like fitted models. A framework that one scripts inside can be licensed or the rates can be completely free.

EXERCISE: Choosing the right software for you

1. Find out the target customers for each of the main types of pricing software.
2. Quantify the benefits, costs and value of your pricing software.
3. Create criteria and processes for choosing the right pricing software for your organisation.

Summary

Choosing the right software and tools is an important decision and one that shouldn't be taken lightly.

The decisions you make now could influence the way your organisation operates for many years, so it's important to always think of the long term. Do not be swayed based only on personal preferences, both yours and from your team, but instead make impartial assessments of the options.

The first option is whether you build a bespoke system or purchase an off-the-shelf tool from a propriety vendor. The available off-the-shelf systems are often easier to manage and have quality tools for audit and management control. Bespoke can be a good choice for some providers, but it depends on the circumstances and objectives of each organisation.

While some rushing to implementation is understandable particularly for new companies or new product lines, in existing companies you should always be aware that choices made might be with you for many years.

Many tools are moving to the cloud, and this is generally a great choice, but it is not without downsides, and you can be left a legacy situation or stuck with a provider when using the cloud. Task management and organisation software has solved many problems with running teams especially for the new operation world of pricing. These are often cost effective and powerful enhancements for a team and department.

10
Looking To The Future

We have now covered the nine different steps in the Price Writer strategy. In this chapter I want you to think about what the future of the insurance pricing industry might look like and what you can do now to future-proof yourself.

New entrants and startups

It's anticipated that many more companies will enter into the insurance space in the future, startups in particular. They can use the intermediary or managing general agent structure to gain a foothold in the sector, which means they do not need the huge amounts of capital required to be insurers straight away but can operate in a similar way selling policies, settling claims and controlling results. There's a pervasive myth about startups in that people think the driver behind them is a lone wolf with a revolutionary idea. This is perhaps true for a small number of companies, but it's mostly false.

If we take Google as an example, when it began it was part of a tapestry of search engines. Google did not come up with the concept of the search engine, it became the most successful because it had a higher relevancy of results. Some search engine providers had focused on giving lots of results and others had focused on providing results quickly, but Google was all about making sure the results were highly relevant and this was the only thing that they were better at doing than their rivals. This is what you see with a lot of successful startups. They're often exactly the same as their competitors or the incumbents, but they're better than their rivals in one particular area and this lines up with what the customer wants or needs. It's this that drives them forward and makes them successful. If a startup can find one small thing that customers care about, and do it better than anyone else, then they'll be able to sell their products.

Incumbents are often unable to compete with startups in that one regard because innovation is hard inside an existing organisation. Those who benefit will stay quiet until the innovation is proven to be successful because they don't want to lose their status, and those who will suffer a disadvantage will immediately shout loudly for exactly the same reason.

Traditionally, pricing techniques have involved the underwriter coming up with their own prices, which were reliant on the individual underwriter's knowledge. In some places, this approach to pricing is still the case, but it will die out almost everywhere. The methods we use now weren't introduced until the 1980s when insurance companies were set up with the aim of removing all the intermediaries and selling direct to the customer. The big example of this is Direct Line. Direct Line wasn't held back by the interests of its existing staff, who would have almost certainly wanted to continue doing things in the way they always had done. Years later, even after they'd grown to become a large organisation, there were still many insurers who had underwriters creating their prices using their own knowledge. It was a real fight to change that culture, even when the success of using the new methods was obvious and proven. This is a war that is not over, but each year we see another area fall to analytics. There is always someone who says such and such area 'is different', only to be wrong again. Rationality will beat subjectivity.

Although the leader of a startup may talk about innovation in all things, that's often not the case because it would be impossible to run a business where you do everything differently. It's almost always the case that they do just one thing differently to their competitors, and that one thing is something customers care about. The important thing to realise is that it's only some customers, not all, who have to care about the thing the startup is better at for the startup to succeed.

Far too often, people dismiss a startup because they don't appreciate what it's trying to do. It's not appealing to the mass market so they don't see the potential; however, this misses the point. To be successful, the startup doesn't need most people to appreciate it, it just needs a small number of people to want the thing it's offering. It's this that provides the oxygen which will help it survive; appealing to the mass market comes much later.

Jeff Bezos of Amazon said, 'Your margin is my opportunity' and it's absolutely true that your inefficiency is someone else's opportunity.[6]

Small companies and freelancers

I'd also expect to see a drive towards more small companies and freelancers becoming involved in this space. When I started out, it was rare to have smaller companies operating within the insurance sector, but we proved our value and there's now a small but growing ecosystem.

This has evolved out of people's individual entrepreneurial drive, their preference to work flexibly for multiple customers and their desire to be in control of their own destiny. The benefit of this for organisations

---

6   S Wu, *Strategy for Executives* (Strategy for Executives, 2019)

is that they can flexibly obtain the skills they need at a particular juncture, or solve problems with outside help and products. This is a way of working that has become normalised and the barriers to selling services to large companies have been breaking down. In the future I expect to see the emergence of more small firms who are specialists in particular things.

Nurturing talent

Your teams need to know and believe in your price strategy and you must live it, breathe it and mean it. Your objectives need to be clear and you need to give people the tools and skills to achieve them while fostering trust, motivating them and leading. Once upon a time, the search for talent and finding quality candidates was a complicated affair of references and endorsements. This is no longer the case and you can now easily share your achievements and knowledge with your colleagues and others in the industry via social media, for example.

Your procedures and processes need to catch up with the new ways, or people will slip through your fingers. You must provide people with ways to develop and recognise the progress they're making. Skills development and qualifications at every stage should be recognised and appropriately rewarded and people's individual progress should be tracked. The training you give people must be relevant to their work and useful to them. Qualifications must be about what people do in their work and clearly linked to what is important for employees, the employer and the end customer. Teaching people things they won't use helps no one and is a waste of time, money and resources.

Qualifications in anything other than the areas people work in and the skills they use to perform their jobs are simply about status and elitism. We are moving into a world where people are trained and qualified in different aspects of GI pricing and they may be certified in particular areas or they might graduate as generalists. Soon the names of functions and products will be the overriding subjects of people's qualifications and people will join you at different levels and demonstrate great attainment. You must be open to all talents from all backgrounds if you want to excel, and the organisations who achieve this will be successful. Anyone who says differently is fighting against the future, and that would put them on the wrong side of history.

Regulatory barriers

Regulatory barriers to entry are also changing. Regulation used to be seen as a substantial barrier to entry, but recently regulators have begun to understand that a vibrant marketplace with multiple providers is better for the customer. In the UK, the regulator insists some products have the same price at new business and renewal, which is known as general insurance price parity (GIPP).

This approach favours new entrants to the marketplace because they can set prices without reference to a back book of policies. It's a regulation that's resulted in the tide going out and the providers who were only surviving through having large margins on their back books have been exposed.

As a result, there has been a small wave of established names exiting from UK GI and a tsunami of small new companies coming in, which proves that those new companies have now got the advantage. GIPPs made it easier for insurers to enter the marketplace and it's likely that other regulators across the world will soon follow suit and introduce similar rules. Although in the short term this approach might disturb the market, in the longer term it's an opportunity and an advantage for us as pricing professionals. More providers means more pricing teams and more price competition and that's a good thing for the people who work in pricing.

What are the big inefficiencies in pricing?

For most of you reading this book, the inefficiencies you're seeing in your organisation are likely to be due to one of these things:

- The structure of your team
- The skills available
- The lack of training options

- Your IT infrastructure

- Your pricing software

- Your price strategy

- Your data set-up

- The resources you have available

One or more of these things will be your Achilles heel and will generate your inefficiencies, and it's in these areas that startups will come along and challenge you. It's particularly easy for them to do so in the area of software because they're not weighed down by having existing software or vested interests in a particular way of doing things. If you're stuck on an existing platform within a legacy provider, then your pricing can weigh you down. Startups will use this to their advantage and can deploy better prices than you because they are faster and more agile.

Unlike established insurers, startups do not have significant amounts of data available to them and this used to be a powerful barrier to entry; however, there are other ways to access this data – for example, from reinsurers and data providers or by scraping the market. If you're an established insurer using legacy software and your people are reluctant to change because that's what they're skilled in, you can see how opportunities for startups emerge.

If you don't do something to address this, you are soon going to see your organisation being eaten away. If you're lucky, you'll have some protection within your distribution method, or your customer base if your customers are loyal to your brand, but this will not last. When this is the case, your loyal customer base probably consists of people who are above the average age and getting older. You're probably not attracting younger people to your product and so it's inevitable that sooner or later you'll start to slide.

Blitz scaling

Blitz scaling is a word that comes from the German word for lightning, *blitz,* and describes the practice of using a huge amount of capital to get a foothold in a particular industry, with the aim of increasing market share and driving out any other form of competition. It is a fast way to build big businesses, such as Uber and Airbnb.

With insurance, this has not been a good strategy, and for the most part those who've tried this approach have failed because insurance is all about capital. The incumbents either have huge amounts of money or they have capacity providers and underwriters with huge amounts of money. They've also got the data, the knowledge, the reputation and everything else that protects them.

You should be aware, though, that capacity providers, underwriters and the people at the start of the chain with those huge amounts of capital to invest can easily switch allegiance and they have no reason to be loyal to anyone. They could happily fund startups and give capacity to them if that will provide them with a good return on their investment. Even providers that are publicly listed can still be taken over by other, larger, companies. Sometimes capacity providers can even end up withdrawing support entirely and this could be seen as an Armageddon for an insurance company.

All this means that startups have an unexpected advantage in the capital areas because while blitz scaling might not work, providers of capital will happily take a risk and switch to startups if doing so requires a relatively small investment to fund. When you're talking about billion-pound capacity providers, they can afford to take that risk and we've seen some big payoffs where that has happened.

Pricing teams and departments

The future of GI pricing is that it's going to be more and more frequently viewed as a multidisciplinary vocation. It will no longer be seen as a remote, scientific branch within a large organisation, but as part of the core operations of the company.

You can expect your teams to become increasingly like those of your colleagues in claims departments: made up of multiple skill sets with a continuum of speciality. Some people within the modern pricing team will be focused on products, and others will be focused on particular functions. You'll have people highly skilled in the subject matters you are insuring, and some people will focus deeply on what you insure, while others will focus deeply on the pricing process or will work together to achieve the objective of charging the exact right price to every customer.

You need to recognise this and provide routes into pricing to people from different backgrounds and at multiple levels. You also need to facilitate and encourage meaningful career progression. You can attract and retain the best people, but you must throw off the veneer of elitism that sadly goes hand in hand with the reputation that insurance is dull. If you don't do these things, you'll never have enough people and you'll never attract the best people.

A friend of mine in IT once told me that the reason why bespoke in-house systems in insurance companies are poor is because insurance IT teams can never attract more than a handful of quality candidates. Great candidates have a wide selection of employers to choose from and will want to find interesting work. Making off-the-shelf software means more transferable skills and a more dynamic workplace, so most of the good candidates do not want to work on making in-house software because it's often tedious and frustrating.

Insurance pricing has not been cursed in the same way: it has always attracted great people and although it may not sound as exciting as other areas, it's far more intellectually stimulating and rewarding. You have to ensure that this continues into the future or you will most certainly lose out.

It's important to remember that what you're doing is intellectually challenging. Trying to work out which events are likely to happen in the future and then decide how much you should charge someone in case those events do happen is difficult. It's not like trying to work out what product to recommend someone on an e-commerce website, or what type of post will attract them on a social media site, or what they should watch on a streaming service – these are all closed systems and it's easy to know if you are successful. People will give you either immediate feedback that you've won or immediate feedback that you haven't.

Our world, the world of insurance, doesn't look like that: it's much more of a grind. It's more difficult to predict outcomes and it's harder to know if we're doing a good job. In addition, we're constantly at war with lots of competitors. In an era when jobs and work are evolving at lightning pace, where what we insure changes constantly and it becomes more necessary to think hard about how the past may not reflect the future, we need to put stock in people who can be agile and develop new skills and work with short timescales. We also need people who show adaptability in their work and thinking. Data coding, programming, testing, forecasting, writing, presenting, listening, designing, troubleshooting, managing, organising, leading, training, teaching – these are the skills we need going forward. They are the skills we need to be fostering in the people who work in our departments and teams, and the skills and experience of pricing managers and pricing project managers in particular will soon become highly sought after.

On my podcast, Outstanding Claims with the Price Writer, I always ask the same three questions: 'How did you get where you are?', 'What's your mission?' and 'What's your vision for the future?' I ask you to consider these now. Gaining clarity on this list is important to understanding yourself, your motivation, and where you are going.

Summary

The future is not going to be like the past. New entrants will exploit our weaknesses because they only need to find one way they are better than incumbents and ensure that is something that customers care about to get traction. We should expect to see more entrants in future, particularly entrants with smaller workforces and a focus on a particular product, channel, or way of doing something. Some will be successful, and they will eat into your market share unless you build an effective pricing team that is not weighed down by inefficiencies. Pricing and other areas of insurance will continue to be supported by contactors and free-lancers and we should expect this to grow, especially because this type of support is becoming more and more normal.

You must nurture talent in your team, and as an industry and specialism we must provide quality opportunities that attract the best talent. Teaching, training and providing qualifications are a very important part of that process. The elitism of paying people based on exams and qualifications that only bear a passing association with the work they actually do in pricing must be consigned to history if we are to attract and keep the best and most talented.

Achieving error-free, quality, accurate and precise deployments time and time again is hard for all, but the greatest organisers and those who can do it and prove their worth will be highly valued and rewarded. If we look at the greatest leads in our organisations, we can see they have highly motivated teams who understand their objectives and strategy.

Conclusion

A typical career lasts 80,000 hours, based on working forty hours per week for fifty weeks of the year for forty years.

The life expectancy today in the UK is eighty years.

The current best estimate for the age of the universe is 13.8 billion years.

If we're lucky enough to reach eighty years old, we will have been breathing for a 172,000,000th of the life of the universe so far. If it were measured in dollars, it would not even be a 1,000th of the size of the greatest fortunes of the richest among us.

I recently visited Wookey Hole Caves. The caves began forming a million years ago, which is a long time, but the Earth is about 4.5 billion years old, so these rock caves and small passages in huge caverns have existed for a 4,500th of the time the Earth has been here. If we transpose the life of the Earth to the eighty years of human life, then these caves would be less than a week old. The point I'm making here is that perspective matters. What seems big in one frame of reference is but a small detail in another, and we should not lose sight of this.

One of the reasons I wrote this book is my own struggle in moving from analyst to leader. At times, I found that transition difficult and although the journey has been richly rewarding for me, both materially and for my mind and soul, it's not been easy. I love what I do and there is a good purpose in my work, but it took me a while to get to a point where I can say that I'm truly happy. My hope with this book is that it helps you to achieve your ambitions in the same way I have achieved mine, but without the struggle and frustrations I experienced.

I recommend that you write down the names of two people you know: one you admire and one you do not. Then work out what you admire about the first person and what you do not admire about the second person. If you emulate the traits and behaviours of the person you admire, and try to avoid the ones in the person you don't, you'll guide your own self-development in a way that will help you to become the best version of yourself.

I know exactly who I admire the most in GI pricing; he is an excellent but, in my view, unsung hero. He runs a team incredibly well, has good judgement and works well with everyone while also achieving his goals and vision. I also know who I admire the least. I try to be like my hero. I try not to be like my anti-hero. Most of the time, I think I succeed, but not all of the time. Just like everyone, I'm a work in progress.

While most of us in pricing work in different companies so are effectively in competition with each other, we are still a community. This means we should share in each other's successes; we should recognise the contributions of those who work for us, with us and elsewhere; we should try to create opportunities for everyone to advance; and we should celebrate each other's wins. Our personal contributions are like ripples on a pond: we can easily see the large impact at the centre, but it's not just about that single event. The energy spreads out across the pool and merges with all the other ripples, and most of the energy is in the outer waves, not those at the centre of the pond. In pricing, we affect many people and we do not even see or know the effects of all that we do.

We should not be motivated by fear of failure. Those who see someone trying hard but not succeeding and who take pleasure from it are not heroes. They're not people we should like or emulate. They're certainly not our friends and we wouldn't want them as colleagues. The people who support us for trying, even when things do not go well, are our best allies. They may never say well done for the things that do not work out, we may never hear from them or know they are even there, but there is an army of people who will support us and who are impressed by the work that we do. We shouldn't forget that. While failure hurts, we should never be embarrassed by it, because we learn more from failure than from anything else.

Again, it's important to have perspective. What we might perceive as a failure might seem like unimaginable success to someone else. They may look upon us and be inspired to try themself; maybe we're the person they want to emulate. That person may even be ourself in the future. All successful people have a string of failures behind them. Trial and error is a totally acceptable way to solve a puzzle and it's also a great way to learn, develop and eventually succeed. Succeeding at something that does not push you and does not cause failure can actually prevent you from succeeding at what you really want to do. You may never end up where you truly belong because you never failed.

With the nine steps I've introduced you to in this book, I have given you the tools you need to succeed in GI pricing. To recap, the steps are:

1. **Strategy** – You've thought about your strategy and how to set yourself up to achieve your objectives.

2. **Enrichment** – You've looked at enrichment and identified the data you need from outside of your own circle to achieve your goals.

3. **Governance** – You've understood that governance is an opportunity because it's your chance to showcase the work you do on a wider stage.

4. **Data** – You've seen how data is the key ingredient to the work you do, and learned why it's important to make sure that it's ready for your team to work on so they don't waste their time on repeated tasks.

5. **Deployment** – You've seen how this is at the centre of the nine steps because it is the moment when all the good work you do reaches your customers and you see the real effect it has.

6. **Capability** – You've thought about how you develop your teams and organise them, and how you manage your people and lead them.

7. **Analysis** – You've looked at analysis and understood why it's such an important part of the nine steps because it allows you day-to-day control over what you're doing and helps you to understand what you should be doing and the impacts of your actions.

8. **Modelling** – You've tested your modelling and learned why it's so important to be able to explain what you're doing to others, including your customers, stakeholders, board members and regulators.

9. **Tools** – You've thought about the way you should be building your infrastructure, what you should have in the way of pricing software, and what you should have in the way of IT infrastructure to ensure your people can do the good work that they need to.

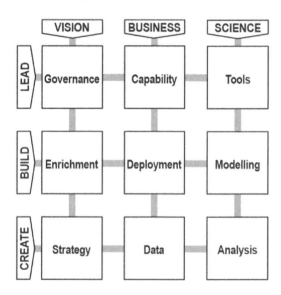

The nine steps are what you need to succeed in your business, and if you follow them, you'll be like the people I admire, the people who are my heroes: those who are leaders in our field, who motivate their teams, who achieve their goals, and who hit their sales and loss ratio targets year after year. You'll work well with other parts of the organisation, and you'll be highly valued and appreciated by all those around you.

This book will get you started so go create, build, lead.

Acknowledgements

There are lots of people who have inspired and taught me. Some know this and others may not.

Let's start with my wonderful wife, two children and all of our family.

Then my bosses and leaders, including Andre Weilert, Chris Legg, Craig Staniland, David Robinson, Fabrice Brossart, Gareth Howell, Graham Ross, Henry de Courtois, Jacqui Draper, Julie Reynolds, Martin Pearce, Stephane Guinet, Waseem Malik, Yves Masson, and first among equals Richard Bretton. You have all helped me to become me.

Next my clients, including Ade Harrison, Ambra Zhang, Amy Gunning, Ashley Lumbard, Charlotte

Ball, Charlotte Halkett, Jack Boult, Jason Cabral, Jay Stewart, Jean-Philippe Doumeng, John Nickson, Jon Craven, Ludo Lacay, Max Bacon, Max Parry, Michalis Antoniou, Paul Smith, Pavel Gertsberg, Rachel Kelsall, Richard Lukeman, Richard Stock, Sam Pratt, Simon Woodhall, Steve Bower, Steve Dobbs, Steven Ball, Stuart Clarke, Stuart Marston, Tom Mansfield and the ever-awesome Gideon Ingham.

There are also many others who made up my teams or who I worked with or alongside. Many will not know just how much they helped and inspired me, including Abigail Clifton, Adrian Clifton, Adrian Lloyd, Adrian Pepper, Aime Lachapelle, Alan Strange, Alan Tabberer, Alex Culora, Alex Veber, Alistair Harper, Alistair Wilkie, Amanda Mason, Amin Abdullah, Amit Patel, Andrea Pollacci, Andy Gee, Anjela Masters, Anthony Drake, Anthony Robinson, Anthony Sanderson, Antoine Paglia, Austin Brislen, Bauke van der Meer, Becky Evans, Bruno Becha, Carlos Remedios, Carlos Thompson, Chris Grant, Chris Phillimore, Chris Tormey, Chris Wakelin, Christopher Hitchins, Clara Pagani, Constance Frécenon, Dave Millington, Deepika Wright, Diane de Reynies, Dom Bird, Domenico Ambrogio, Ed Sutton, Emma Pritchard, Esther Villar Jimenez, Evan Waks, Farran Florne, Faye Jones, Fleur Le Carpentier, Gareth Atkins, Gareth Davies, Gaurav Vaidya, Giovanni Ciampa, Greg Marshall, Guillaume Beraud-Sudreau, Hannah Doran, Harish Iyer, Harriet Rees, Hazel Davis, Ian Forbes, Isabelle Hirst, Jack Herklots, James

Harward, James Owen, Jamie Glover, Jason Eatock, Jess Maisey, Jimmy Hill, Joanna Chardon, Joe Rivers, Joost van Bruggen, Joseph Sherratt, Justin Belgrove, Kate Handford, Katy Edwards, Katy Wiltshire, Kevin Vu, Kinga Kita, Kirsten Britland, Kitty Deane, Kristina Ivatovic, Lisa Evans, Liz Thompson, Luca Toscani, Mallika Natarajan, Mark Rhodes, Marco Chianese, Martin Pullan, Martyn Stimson, Mary Webb, Matt Draisey, Matt Wright, Matthew Walley, Mike Ransom, Nick Alvis, Nick Porter, Nicola Firth, Nicola Parkinson, Nicolas Bosc, Nicolas Hebrant, Paul Frith, Paul Goswamy, Paul Leck, Raj Lakhani, Ralph Clayton, Reuven Shnaps, Roman Bryl, Sainish Sharma, Sam Day, Sam Packwood, Sarah Campbell, Sarah Vaughan, Scott Chattin, Shameema Bonomaully, Sirisha Gopireddy, Terry Yip, Tom Clarke, Tom Kavanagh, Tom Saliba, Tom Snowdon, Trevinder Thandi, Vishal Patel, Wayne Damant, Xavier Chassagnol, especially Yiannis Parizas, and everyone else I have worked with over the years.

Also, a thank you to those who read this book first, including Andy Cooper, Catrin Townsend, Dawid Kopczyk, James Hillon and Ronald Richman.

And finally a huge thank you to my absolute hero Arnold Schwarzenegger.

The Author

Jeremy Keating is the co-founder of Price Writers, an offshoot of his consultancy, Price Writer. Price Writers is a training and events company in general insurance pricing. Jeremy started in GI pricing in 2009, and since that time he has gone from analyst to pricing leader, with all the ups and downs that involves. He has worked with many companies and many more have attended his Price Writers events, including the AA, Admiral, Ageas, Agria, AIG, Allianz, Animal Friends, Ardonagh Group, Apollo, Aviva, AXA, Bupa, Chubb, Direct Line Group, Earnix, Esure, Equifax, Experian, EY, First Central, Fluffy, Guy Carpenter, Hellas Direct,

Hiscox, Homeprotect, Hymans Robertson, Intelligent Insurance, Juniper, KPMG, LexisNexis, Liberty Mutual, Lloyds Banking Group, Lombard, Many Pets, Markerstudy Group, Markel, Maven Blue, Medical Protection Society, Moodys, Munich Re, Napo, NFU Mutual, Octo Telematics, Old Mutual, Policy Expert, Prestige Underwriting, Prima, Quantee, Sainsbury's Bank, Skyblu, Somerset Bridge Group, Sophro, Staysure, Swiss Re, Tedaisy, Tawuniya, Qmetric Group and Vitality.

When Jeremy was first promoted to manager, he was excited to be gaining the success he desperately craved, but he found the change in his role difficult and disorientating. There was so much he didn't know, and none of the learning and training was about the problems he had: either it was so general that it was useless for being a leader in a technical role or it was super specific on technical work. Jeremy struggled in the role, and it took him a long time to find his feet and become the leader he is today.

Jeremy wants other pricing leaders to become the most successful and highly valued leaders in general insurance. He does not want others to struggle like he did. He wants to provide the knowledge and skills needed for them to excel with training that is about the work they actually do. Jeremy wants every pricing leader to reach the level that matches their ambition. He doesn't want anyone to give up early with their potential unfulfilled.

Jeremy also wants every customer to pay the exact right price with no technical constraints, barriers or errors. What he calls the 'Goldilocks price', the price that's just right. This price is different for each provider and product and is the price that exactly matches each customer to the provider's strategy and position – allowing customers the full benefit of price competition based on the merits of each offering.

Jeremy and Price Writers offer training programmes. To read more about this or to connect with Jeremy, please visit the websites.

⊕ www.PriceWriters.com

⊕ www.linkedin.com/in/Jeremy-Keating

Printed in Great Britain
by Amazon

38964968R00121